Support Social Development

Positive Relationships in the Early Years

by Jennie Lindon

Updated to reflect the 2012 EYFS

Published by Practical Pre-School Books, A Division of MA Education Ltd, St Jude's Church, Dulwich Road, Herne Hill, London, SE24 0PB.
Tel: 020 7738 5454 www.practicalpreschoolbooks.com

© MA Education Ltd 2011. Revised edition 2013. Illustrations by Cathy Hughes. Front cover image photo taken by Lucie Carlier © MA Education Ltd.

ISBN 978-1-909280-25-0

Social development over early childhood

National early years frameworks around the UK give a prominent place to personal, social and emotional development (PSED), including patterns of social behaviour and the growth of empathy. The revised Early Years Foundation Stage (for England) has retained an emphasis on positive relationships through 'Making relationships'. This focus is present in descriptive material about two-year-olds and forms one of the early learning goals for PSED.

All the early years national frameworks imply that thoughtful practitioners, and their provision, will support children. However, there is not much detail about what actually helps babies and children to flourish socially – or what could undermine them. Young children do not make close, personal relationships with other children, unless circumstances are favourable to this development. Positive social development does not just happen. Certainly, adults do not promote friendly behaviour between children, or actual friendships, simply by announcing "We're all friends here".

What often seems to be missing in discussions about social development is a strong focus on the perspective of the young child. Best practice has a strong element of looking through children's eyes about how the seeds of possible friendship are sown and how friendships become strong – or fade. The starting point in looking at children's social development is grounded in the firm foundations of practitioners' knowledge about child development. There are plenty of pointers to help this process, and this section focuses on how babies and young children develop socially.

The social baby and toddler

In the normal course of events, babies are born social. Their ears are attuned to the sound of the human voice and their brains are poised to process spoken language. Human infants are physically uncoordinated and they need a huge amount of care in comparison with other very young mammals. They cannot scamper after their family like a little lamb, to insist on social and close physical contact. Instead, human babies use their eyes and other senses like touch to communicate. In particular, babies use a steady stare to communicate by locking onto the eyes and face of others. They also use their voice, in communication that steadily moves from crying to a wide range of sounds.

Responsiveness to familiar adults

Throughout the first year of life, babies are responsive to the sounds of familiar adults and children, including their siblings. Parents or early years practitioners should become uneasy when a baby seems unresponsive to a smiling face, affectionate touch or the sounds of human speech. Babies all have their own temperament, and some are by nature more lively in actions and sound making. However, there is good reason to be concerned when babies are unresponsive, rather than simply quiet, or slower to warm up than their peers within a playful exchange with a familiar adult or child.

The crucial beginnings of social interaction are established over the baby year. Babies become ever more social as the direct result of generous personal attention from a few adults, with whom they become very familiar. Suitable playthings are important for babies, but toys can never in themselves promote sociability in the very young. By the end of their first year, older babies can be active participants in conversational-type exchanges because of all their experiences that support social learning over infancy. They become able to pay attention – looking and listening in the way that older babies and young toddler are able to – with familiar adults. They hold a mutual gaze and use pointing, as well as looking, to direct your attention towards something of interest. In a slightly different way, babies also gain social experiences from affectionate contact with siblings and other slightly older children.

Older babies and young toddlers can have the building blocks for conversation long before they speak recognisable words. The give-and-take of reciprocal communication is an essential part of social contact. Watch nearly one-year-olds, who have had sufficient personal interaction over the baby year. You see the looking, pausing and expectant expression that are just as much part of friendly contact as the sound making and speech-like flow that comes before spoken language.

Responsiveness to other children

Very young children do not only make friendly contact with familiar adults. Babies and toddlers show that they recognise familiar peers and, within their physical abilities, engage in social play with individuals. Even the very youngest children are aware of each other and alert adults can see those early social contacts. Babies and very young toddlers, who spend enough time together regularly, get to know each other on a friendly basis. You will see their face light up in recognition and even babies, who are familiar with each other, will stare or put out a hand to touch each other.

Walking older babies, and definitely toddlers, engage in social play by establishing a joint focus of interest. For instance, they make physical contact with an object that another young child (or an adult) is holding and manipulating. The action communicates non-verbally that 'I'm interested too'. There is also a lot of deliberate imitation of what the other child (or the adult) does. This copying action again sends a non-verbal message along the lines of 'I like this too' and 'how about we do it together?'.

Look closer: making contact through play

In Little Learners Nursery School the base room for older toddlers and young twos is called 'The Snug'. There are low mirrors fixed to the wall at child height. Mirrors are a valuable addition to any setting, as they are often used by children in joint activity: looking at each other as well as themselves in the mirror. On the day of my visit, the under twos were busily engaged in a range of activities (examples later) but I only saw them briefly at the mirrors.

The nursery shared with me two recent observations that showed this opportunity in action. James (15 months) loves dressing up and during this day he chose a hat and went to look in the mirror. Freddy (22 months) saw what James

Links to your practice

Within their own family, babies make active contact with parents and other close relatives. Some babies spend considerable time in non-family care, in a day nursery or the home of a childminder. It is essential that the key person in the group setting, or the childminder, welcomes personal contact with individual babies, developing a close and affectionate relationship with them (Lindon, 2012b). Wherever they spend their days, babies and young toddlers – slightly older children too – need the emotional security that comes from a close attachment to a small number of familiar adults.

In what ways have you explored, and ensured, that your key person approach ensures babies and young children can make a personal, close relationship from which they can then choose to make broader social contacts?

had done, fetched a hat for himself and joined James at the mirror. These two very young children spent time smiling and laughing at each other. They sat comfortably, both of them at the mirror, carefully observed and deliberately imitated each other's play movements.

In another observation Lizzie and Edward – both two years of age – were playing in the den that had been built. The practitioner turned the mirrored shelves around so that the mirror faced into the den. Lizzie and Edward (who are very close friends) sat in the small space, pointed to the mirror and laughed at each other. The practitioner joined the children and pulled a face herself. The children then copied her and had fun sticking out their tongues, seeing the reflection in the mirror and laughing loudly. The two children continued to track each other's actions. They imitated specific movements and sounds from the other child. The practitioner stayed with Lizzie and Edward and added her contribution by offering brief comments on what they were doing.

Toddlers' interest in mirrors has often started when they were much younger. The team in the 'Baby Nest' room regularly see babies, who are comfortable to lay on their tummies, looking closely at the wall mirror in that room. Individual babies often explore what they see with their hands by tapping the mirror. They look unsure, but also excited, by their reflection.

A very normal problem for the very youngest children is that sometimes their attempts to make social contact do not go smoothly. Babies' and toddlers' social moves are often more physical. They can hurt without any deliberate intention, because their strategy for gaining another's attention may be to seize hold of a fistful of hair or another little arm. A touch turns into an unintentional push, or a full body wrestle, which is not always welcomed by the toddler on the receiving end. A very vigorous

It is worthwhile thinking why the social moves of older babies, toddlers and young twos are sometimes overlooked by adults. What do you think about the following possibilities?

- Perhaps very early social behaviour is semi-dismissed by early years practitioners, if they have been encouraged to view what they see and hear as 'just parallel play' or 'only playing alongside each other'.

- Some adults do not welcome some of the actions involved in toddlers' reciprocal game play that involve imitation. Practitioners, and parents too, may look askance at cooperative bouncing up and down on the sofa, or perfect turn taking to post small toys down the drain. You may need to re-direct the shared focus of these toddlers or two-year-olds. Nevertheless, what you saw was genuine social play and friendly interaction.

- Sometimes you need to deal with the physical fall-out of more exuberant play. Again, socially sensitive adults recognise that, until the unfortunate crash of buggies (or two little heads), these young twos were engaged in intense social interaction, supported by their chosen dollies and buggies.

- Is the adults' attention most caught by the genuine struggle for very young children with taking turns over play resources? It does not matter how many bags you have, at some point two toddlers (or slightly older children too) will insist on their territorial rights over the same bright red handbag.

- Yet, the same toddlers or young twos manage well with turn taking over actions: for instance the sequence of "I peep at you and then you peep at me and then I…". Is this observation less prominent in adult memory – or documentation – than the handbag fight?

hug may result in both toddlers toppling over – not necessarily with any physical damage, but it can be a close thing. The communicative touch on a toy, to initiate play, may be interpreted by the other child as an attempt to seize the item. The first child reacts by holding on harder, or glares with the message of 'get off it!'.

Of course, one- and two-year-olds do not play in the same way as slightly older children. They do already make active social moves which can develop into the initiation of social games with familiar children, as well as adults. Babies and young toddlers' sociability involves a lot of looking and moving alongside, but in their own way they are active in making this contact. Twos, and some older toddlers, begin to be able to

coordinate their actions towards new play sequences, just as much as they add to existing play rituals. They use verbal and non-verbal communication to guide the interaction, and these skills are sometimes used by a younger child to initiate a familiar pattern of play with an older child, perhaps a sibling. You can find family examples in Dunn (1984) and Lindon (2012c).

Very young children cannot yet manage the complex pretend play that is within the scope of mainly threes and fours. However, they enthusiastically accept minor walk-on parts, when welcomed by older siblings or other familiar children. Under-threes, even under-twos, are willing to tolerate a fair amount of being ordered about by four-year-old play directors, so long as the younger ones are allowed to join the pretend dragon hunt, or sit in the beach café. Such opportunities are only available to the youngest children if they spend at least some of their day, or part of the week, in a mixed-age range. If their social interaction is always within a narrow age band of under-twos or threes, they will not get these opportunities. See the discussion on page 28 about ways to bring different ages together.

The social and emotional child

Twos and threes are increasingly able to draw on their spoken language skills to make personal contact with peers, to share interests in a simple way and to make suggestions within chosen play. These still young children are able to use verbal, as well as non-verbal, means of communication to show and gain attention and to support a friendly atmosphere of responsiveness within play and other joint enterprises.

Claire Vallotton and Catherine Ayoub (2010) observed very young children at 14, 24 and 36 months of age and tracked how their growing vocabulary enabled the children to be adept at self-regulation. The number of different words that young children used was more significant than sheer talkativeness: how much they said in total. Young children's growing ability to express out loud their wishes, preferences and feelings means that they are more able to adjust their own behaviour – in a simple way – to the social situation.

As children's language develops, some of their vocabulary may enable them to express what they feel through words. Of course, babies show their feelings: contentment as well as distress, happy recognition as well as surprise or wariness. Throughout the second year of life toddlers are making sense of spoken language and learning that people, objects and actions can be represented by words. Once they have this basis, then over the year that they are two, young children are able to learn words to name and express feelings like being happy or cross. They initially apply these words to their own feelings, but steadily very young children start to suggest that someone else is 'sad'. Like any other extension to their vocabulary, young children need to hear the words for feelings in context. If their familiar adults do not use an emotional vocabulary in a meaningful way, then children cannot pluck words out of the air.

Clearly, adults and children experience a far wider range of feelings than these six emotions. The very practical point is that, without verbal communication – asking and explaining – the chances of being accurate in reading embarrassment, anxiety, guilt, jealousy and so on, are very much reduced. Children learn about many feelings through social interaction. The ability to talk and listen to the reply is a crucial part of this development.

Young children do not only learn the words to name feelings. They absorb broad social messages. For instance, over early and middle childhood, girls and boys learn whether feeling 'guilty' is an important concept in their family or broader cultural group. They realise that some feelings are more welcome to their familiar adults: maybe everyone is supposed to 'put on your happy face'. Perhaps the expression of distress or anxiety gets a different response, depending on whether you are a girl or a boy. Young children also learn about acceptable and unwelcome ways of expressing feelings like anger or frustration.

Choice over expression of emotions

Over early childhood, young girls and boys are able, with some help, to learn active control of their emotions. They become able to hold back a little on their impulse to unleash angry or distressed feelings in ways that hurt other people. Nancy Eisenberg (1992) makes a persuasive case that this self-regulation over emotions is the basis for children's repertoire of skills that ease their social interaction. Friendly contact between children and social play is

Understanding emotions

The social world of feelings is a confusing place – think about how adults sometimes misread the emotion felt by a fellow-adult, even a person they know very well. In an uncertain or puzzling situation, young children will sometimes turn towards a familiar adult (parent or key person), to look at her or his reaction. This process, called emotional or social referencing, is a strategy that seems to reassure children. 'Does my Daddy look comfortable about this loud stranger with the tambourine? Yes, he looks cheerful, maybe I will start singing along too.' Or 'whoops, Daddy has got his frowny face, I am right to feel I would much rather be somewhere else'.

Young children are certainly not going to be more accurate than adults in reading the emotions of other people. It seems that grown-ups, across diverse cultures, are largely correct in interpreting four emotions exclusively from body language, including facial expression. These basic emotions are fear, anger, happiness and sadness. A further two emotions – surprise and disgust – are often, but not always, interpreted correctly by non-verbal means. These findings come from the cross-cultural research of Paul Ekman, and are summarised with reference to children by Helen Bee and Denise Boyd (2004).

Links to your practice

Listen to twos and young threes that you know. What words do they use to refer to feelings? The point here is to be alert to what children choose to say, without any prompting from you. Consider what they express in the context of their relationships with other children – or possibly linked with their favourite stories in their own spontaneous comments about characters.

Do you work with three- or four-year-olds who rarely or never use words to name and describe feelings? How often do they hear this kind of emotional vocabulary, as part of a timely comment from you, applied to real events?

These comments and questions apply equally to young boys as to girls. There is good reason to challenge any implication that boys are less sensitive to emotions than girls. Lise Eliot (2009, pages 253-6) points out that the sensitivity of very young males usually leads them to conclude that they are not supposed to express certain feelings. A circular effect is also set in place whereby, if adults comment less to boys about emotions within spontaneous events, then boys get less experience than girls about putting feelings into spoken words.

supported when children are able and willing to allow for 'you first' sometimes, rather than always 'me first'. Children can also be motivated to find ways to express emotions that do not annoy their companions and lead to the temporary disruption of play.

Young children can learn self-regulation with adult help. It would be unrealistic to expect under-threes to hold back; they tend to express straightaway whatever emotion is uppermost. However, wise adults have started the process of guiding toddlers' actions, when their chosen way of expressing feelings is going to hurt somebody. Older threes, and increasingly the fours and fives, become more able – at least sometimes – to inhibit the expression of strong feelings, when they judge it is neither the time nor the place. Adults are sometimes, understandably, most concerned about physical expressions of anger. However, by the end of early childhood five- and six-year-olds can be irritated by peers whose main option for expressing frustration, or even mild sadness, is to burst into tears.

Friendships over early childhood

Virginia Buysse and her colleagues (2002) point out that different branches of psychology have tended to sub-divide social relationships over childhood in ways that reflect the adults' study interests. It is less usual to have a focus that starts with how children most likely view their social world. A complicating factor is that some research has depended on parents or teachers saying which children are friends – not always an accurate way forward.

Kind and playful adults make a huge difference for a happy childhood. But children relate to other children in a different way – for talk, play, exploration or just companionable sitting and watching the world go by. Listen and you will hear children playing with language in repetitive and sing-song ways that they realise

Food for thought

It has generally been a positive move for early years practitioners to avoid the unhelpful labels of 'good', 'bad' or 'naughty'. A popular alternative has emerged of using 'inappropriate' and 'appropriate' behaviour. This choice brings some problems, when used as a shorthand about the ground rules around friendly interaction or ways to express feelings under pressure which are welcomed, or not, by the adults.

When terming a child's behaviour 'inappropriate' it is worth reflecting on who thinks this choice of behaviour is 'inappropriate' and why? The adults need to be clear about what underlies their judgement and how they can make this understandable to a young child.

Just as important, is how do you show, and tell, young children why a different reaction, to the same tricky social situation, is a better choice to make?

even the most lively adult does not want to continue with for ages. Threes and fours spend time giggling about topics (like poo) which they have realised adults do not find very funny. They enjoy re-running their preferred games or pretend play themes in ways that even the most thoughtful of grown-ups are tempted to try to 'improve'. In a happy atmosphere with enough resources, children are sometimes pleased to be left in peace with each other.

What is friendship?

Judy Dunn has undertaken a considerable amount of observational research into family life and interaction between siblings. In *Children's Friendships* (2004) she turned her attention to the relationships that are forged between unrelated children. Books about friendship often start with primary school and middle childhood, but Judy Dunn describes how the close and caring relationship that characterises friendship, can definitely develop over early childhood. She makes a strong case (with which I agree) that friendship is reciprocal – both parties feel and agree that 'we are friends' and that applies to young children's friendships just as much as in later life.

Marion Dowling (2005) summarises research showing the importance to children of their chosen friendships. It is not at

all surprising that children experience happier transitions when they move on with the company of friends. Children express regret for the loss of friends when they have split up to go to different reception classes. Other disruptions happen as the consequence of several moves between settings for young children over early childhood. All the nurseries I have visited (for this and other books) gave serious consideration to friendship patterns in the timing of internal transitions, when children moved into the next age-based room.

Marion Dowling accurately points out that three-year-olds tend to regard their current playmates as their 'friends', even though this social relationship may be temporary. I would add that young children's easy use of the word may simply echo how their familiar adults talk to them. It is not unusual for parents and practitioners to say: "There's your friend" in reference to a peer that this child has only met once before. Maybe the apparent greater stability of four- and five-year-olds over friendships is at least partly children's growing ability to correct adults with: "She (or he) is not my friend".

It is a challenge to thoughtful adults to unravel what aspects of young social contact can be attributed mainly to their stage of development. A confusing factor is that young children are dependent on adults for the pool from which they can choose friends. Descriptions of social development sometimes imply that, in contrast with older children, young friendships are more transitory. Yet some threes or fours have not chosen to lose their friends by switching to a different nursery, or because one family relocates out of the neighbourhood.

> ### How do children make friends?

It is something of a challenge for adults to gain an accurate insight into how friendships develop for young children. Susan Danby (in Brooker and Woodhead, 2008) points out that very little research has focused on how young children actually manage their friendships. Friendly social interaction has often been explored by interviews or examples that capture a snapshot of what is happening. These descriptions are useful, but, I would agree that sometimes it is hard to put aside adult interpretations and focus on children's likely perspective. A key issue for young children is how they meet other young girls or boys who might be welcome play companions and some could later become friends.

Young girls and boys need to have contact with other children – an obvious point but important not to overlook. Young children are dependent on adults for their range of potential friends and the likely sources include the following:

- The close and extended family: young children may spend a lot of time with, and feel friendly towards, children to whom they are related. You could say that siblings or cousins are a different kind of friend.

- The immediate neighbourhood and the extent to which children come together in each other's homes or gardens.

Food for thought

As well as considering the developmental side to social relationships, it is useful to reflect on what we as adults think about friendship between children. What leads us to say that two children are 'friends'? How do these children behave with each other that leads us to this conclusion? Do we actually think enough about our reasons for deciding that individual young girls and boys are friends with other individual children?

- How do you and your colleagues decide that young children are friends?

- Are you tempted to tell children that they are 'friends'? How would you feel if a fellow-adult did this to you?

- Do children have acquaintances, with whom they may be friendly, but these children are not friends?

Food for thought

Think back over your own childhood. Look at the suggestions in this section and recall the sources of your own friendships in early childhood.

- What drew you to some children so that both of you became friendly?

- Did you have no choice but to spend time with some children, whom you would never have chosen as friends?

- What insights can you now bring to your time as an adult with young children?

- The children of their parents' friends, because the families spend time together.

This youngest generation also meets other children through their attendance at some kind of early years provision. Group provision, but also the home of a childminder, offers a wider choice for potential playmates and close friends than is likely from even a large family and neighbourhood social life.

Look closer: the support of a home-like environment

Red Hen Day Nursery

Considerable thought has gone into the physical environment of this nursery. The indoor areas are organised with smaller, cosy spaces, as well as through

routes and more open areas. It is easy for children to gather together with friends, when and how they wish. The adults are easily available for play and conversation, but there is a confidence in the team that children need time to be together, without an adult always being very close.

There were comfortable seating areas indoors, where it was easy for a few children to settle companionably, with or without an adult. But the outdoor courtyard also had seating areas made comfortable with substantial outdoor beanbags, which easily seated an adult with two children. A large tyre offered another option for sitting together in the courtyard garden.

Indoors and outside there were a range of options for a couple of children to be cosy together. In the home base room for twos a range of comfortable spaces also includes a little house type space with a cushioned base and the possibility of letting down curtains to make an enclosed space for a few children.

Little pop-up tents and a good choice of large cardboard boxes were used by children and adults. At one point in the garden a practitioner was sitting in one cardboard

box with a hula-hoop as a wheel. Other children were in nearby boxes in a pretend game which involved travelling in space, but changed as time passed.

Look closer: Little Learners Nursery School

Equal thought has gone into the learning environment here. For instance, the older toddlers and younger twos have the home base of 'The Snug'. This area has been organised in ways that enable these very young children to come together easily, as and when they wish, and with the discreet support of friendly adults. The room is resourced by plenty of baskets and other containers and this indoor environment has several choices for children to sit together out of choice, to be quiet companions, enjoy a book or two or sit and look out over the room.

The home and cooking area is equipped with metal plates, rather than plastic. Like other thoughtful teams, Little Learners aims to reduce the use of plastic in the learning environment to occasions when plastic truly is the best or only material for the job. The fruit and vegetables for pretend cooking are real items of food, which obviously are refreshed at regular intervals. These very young children can organise themselves by selecting from the materials. I watched as one adult and two girls were in this area. One girl was busy organising the plates in the pretend kitchen. The second girl was looking on and the adult sitting with her was commenting quietly on the play. But this practitioner was also using the names of other children on a regular basis, to support this child who was new to the group.

The Little Explorers Room (older twos and threes) also has a dedicated home corner with real food. For these slightly older children, the plates are proper crockery and the cutlery is real. Children take care and there have been no breakages. The Pre-School Room (older threes and fours) also has a child-sized real kitchen in a side room where children are able to do cooking. They also take the real food to be cooked in the outdoor fire pit (see the example on page 10).

> Friendships need time to develop

It is handy to consider what circumstances children need in order to establish friendly relationships with other children, to choose temporary playmates and have the opportunity to decide with whom they want to spend much of their time – to become friends and consolidate those friendships. I think the main issues are time and regular contact, in an environment that is not over-organised by the adults.

Children – young and older – may warm to each other on first meeting, but they are not instant friends. Promising potential friendships cannot take root if girls and boys have no idea when, or if, they will meet up again. On the contrary, children who meet regularly, even if not every day, are able to anticipate seeing a child who has become a friend and they recall what they enjoy doing together.

- Children need time to become familiar with each other – at the basic level to recognise each other by face, and for the twos and older, by personal name.

- They need this time to get to know each other as individuals within a pattern of regular contact.

- As well as sustained periods of time, children need space and an environment that enables them to discover shared interests.

- A great deal happens through play and playful pursuits, but a common, age-appropriate fluent language is also important. Threes and fours like to talk about their interests, likes and dislikes.

- Children, like their older counterparts, often bond over something they have in common: a shared passion for dinosaurs, dressing up as fairies, digging holes or a consuming interest in a fictional character, from a book, DVD or the television.

Look closer: simple talk to organise play

In Red Hen Day Nursery, like the other settings mentioned in examples, children have considerable choice about where and when to play, and their choice of companions.

I watched Jack and Rory (both 2yrs, 8mths) who were busy with a child-sized umbrella, which belonged to Jack. They were taking a break from playing together on the wheeled vehicles in the courtyard garden to try to get the umbrella to go up. Jack suggested to Rory: "You help me do it, then I will play with you". Rory agreed immediately and, with the two of them working on the problem, they succeeded and then returned to the vehicles.

I talked with a practitioner who explained that these two boys had until recently been part of a group of three friends. The eldest had moved into the Kindergarten room, and the dynamics of this little group had changed. Today was the first day that Jack and Rory had played together without the third companion present.

Developing social sensitivity

Young children grow in their understanding of their social world. However, there are limits to the ability of young children to manage the subtle issues that arise in social interaction. As children's spoken language increases, adults' expectations over behaviour, like sharing, sometimes take an unwarranted leap forward.

Emotional literacy

The social sensitivity of 'emotional literacy', and the behaviour classed as social skills, are sometimes bundled up together. These two broad areas are both important, but in rather different ways. Genuinely helpful adults set their expectations of young children at a developmentally realistic level. They also recognise that sensitivity and the range of skills are not taught, as if they are a school subject. Children's personal, social and emotional development unfolds through their daily experiences, and the sense that they make of them.

Emotional literacy means the ability to express your own feelings and to recognise the possible impact of those emotions on other people. The other side of the coin is the ability to understand what other people may be feeling: their invisible, internal state which they express in words or behaviour. Young children will not grow in emotional literacy unless they feel emotionally secure. If children's lives are unpredictable, young boys and girls will be fully absorbed trying to understand what on earth is happening now, or avoiding emotionally harsh adults. They will be far too busy with self-protection to have any energy to spare for the feelings and wishes of any of their peers.

Social skills are behaviours that generally promote harmony within groups. Examples include learning to take turns or taking a problem-solving approach to disagreements. These behaviours are linked with skills of social communication, such as willingness to listen to others, rather than interrupt, as well as express your own view. Again, it is only within an emotionally warm environment that young children will have the spare energy and motivation to give way sometimes to the needs of others.

Socially sensitive patterns of behaviour make life considerably easier for children in group interaction and for the responsible adults. The actions can be linked with a pro-social pattern, rather than anti-social behaviour. But it is handy to realise that social skills, just like alert understanding of the feelings of other people, can be used in different ways. Children learn about the moral, or ethical, undertones of social behaviour. If children understand what matters to a peer or sibling, then that knowledge can be used to support – but it can also be used to tease and annoy. Even 'nice' children will do this sometimes and emotionally fragile children may learn to feel better by making someone else feel worse.

Helpful adults ease the social situation

Undoubtedly, life in the social group of a nursery or the family home of a childminder is calmer and more enjoyable for everyone when young children progress on the learning journey for the behaviours under the broad umbrella of 'sharing'. This broad (adult) concept includes taking turns on limited resources, accepting that another child can play with the cars (and other possessions in common) and recognising that you cannot always have first call on the time and attention of favourite grown-ups. Young children are able to develop these abilities and lay down habits of behaviour that help social interaction within small groups. However, they do not progress in these ways just because the months and years have passed.

A considerable amount depends on experiences over early childhood. A significant part is contributed by familiar adults in the child's life, including whether they hold realistic expectations of what young age groups are likely to manage. The additional adult responsibility is to set a consistently good example to children. In my visits to early years settings I have observed courteous and thoughtful young children, who were very happy to apply those social skills to a visitor. Always, as my day passed in the nursery or centre, I could see that these children had positive role models in their practitioners. They did not spend their days telling children to be 'kind'; those adults behaved in ways that showed kindness, and other qualities, in action. The children may also, of course, have had similar good examples to imitate from their own family life.

Look closer: waiting and taking turns for a good reason

Little Learners Nursery School has an outdoor fire pit. This permanent feature is a recessed circular area with a grid over the top for cooking when it is operational, and a full cover when the pit has cooled down. An adult is always present when the pit is working. An outer circle of tree stumps provides seating and a visual reminder about keeping back from the pit. I watched during the morning when potatoes were being baked and a kettle was regularly boiling on the grid, ready for hot chocolate. Children were also toasting marshmallows using long sticks.

It was striking that these young children, varying in age from two to four years, were very able to wait and take turns. These social skills, which in some circumstances seem to be such a struggle, were being used with ease. There was a calm, focused atmosphere around this resource, as with other areas of the garden. Children looked relaxed, confident that everyone would get their turn. The fire pit was working for much of the morning, so there was no rush.

The practitioner who was responsible for the fire pit was relaxed in her turn and a lot of conversation just flowed as some children toasted their marshmallows. Children fetched their own mug and spoon from their indoor kitchen and were happy to wait a short while, if necessary, for their turn to add the chocolate powder to milk in their mug, then stir after the adult added the hot water from the kettle. Children then sat on a tree stump seat and sipped their drink. Sometimes, children were happy to sit and wait (or return later) because the adult pointed out that the kettle needed to boil again.

Children sat and chatted as they sipped. These slightly older children knew each other well and it was noticeable how they greeted each other and the adults by name. One boy (four-years-old) welcomed the nursery manager, who came to join the informal group, and offered to mix a hot chocolate especially for her – which he did.

> Sibling relationships

Friendly relationships do not always go smoothly – even between grown-ups. Adults need to bear this point in mind when looking at the ability and willingness of young children to be attentive to the needs of others and to cooperate in socially sensitive behaviour. Claire Hughes (2011) offers some insights from a study of relationships (undertaken with Judy Dunn) between siblings, from when the younger child was aged two up to six years. Sibling relationships are not the same as friendships, not least because you never chose your siblings. However, I think there are some useful pointers from the study – see what you think.

The study confirmed findings from previous family studies (Dunn, 1984; 1993) that younger children extend their understanding of feelings, behaviour and the connection between the two as the result of bickering and teasing between siblings. This kind of low conflict can bring intervention by parents and a similar situation often operates in early years provision. Adults think they should enter on the side of the child who seems to be losing. Yet, careful listening sometimes tells you this is an equal struggle, which does not need your help, at least at the moment.

Claire Hughes' study emphasises that children often sort out temporary bickering or wind-ups without help. They are motivated to resolve it quickly, because they want to get back to play. She suggests also that the younger siblings learn to assert themselves and that their language is positively supported by their strong motivation to make their point in a dispute. In the family, or elsewhere, it is a different situation if children are engaged in long-term, bitter argument and rivalry. Claire Hughes (again like Judy Dunn in her earlier studies) documented how much younger children gain from being involved in long-running games, often pretend, with their sibling.

Complications for social development

Young children are usually motivated to make social contact and their efforts can overcome some potential obstacles. It is also important for adults to recall that children, like grown-ups, have different temperaments. Not all children want a very active social life. Some like peace and quiet and are not necessarily lonely when they choose to be alone. Careful adult judgement of whether children need some help, is based on equally careful observation of what is actually is or is not happening between children.

Even socially-minded children may have off-days and your attention should be caught by individual children who are uncharacteristically quiet. They may be worried about something and want to confide in a private conversation. They may be unwell or tired. Children's physical well-being is likely to affect their sociability, and perhaps make them less patient towards their peers. Anecdotal evidence from early years teams suggests that some young children do not have a peaceful bedtime routine and enough sleep for their psychological well-being. Children who are cranky out of semi-permanent exhaustion are unlikely to be happy playmates.

Minimal contact with other children

Children generally relate to adults in different ways to how they talk and play with other children. So, it can be perplexing for children when they meet with peers, if they have otherwise spent most of their time with adults in their own family. It is important not to build a general theory out of anecdotal information. However, I have encountered quite a few examples of two- to four-year-olds who seemed confused about the ground rules in a child's world, with which their peers were relatively at ease. The shared feature was lack of contact with other children and not the possibility of a disability that could affect social development.

Skills for relating to other children

In favourable circumstances, children learn over early childhood the practical skills of social communication and how to be a

---

Food for thought

Claire Hughes' study is aligned with approaches like the HighScope approach on conflict resolution (Evans, 2002). Children cannot learn to resolve the normal ups and downs of daily life, if adults always rush to sort out and smooth over any problems.

I think it is also important to avoid labelling even minor rudeness between children as 'bullying'. Of course, it matters if children target others in a sustained and deliberate way, with understanding of the consequence of their behaviour (Lindon, 2012d).

It is especially poor practice to label very young children as 'bullies', because the term implies that they have the ability to plot and foresee the impact of their actions. Attentive adults need to avoid a punitive approach and instead to: listen, help young children to make amends and, just as important, have some grasp of the different choice to make next time.

Links to your practice

Young children are less attractive play companions to other young boys and girls if, for instance, they refuse to join in pretend play, because it is not real and therefore 'silly'. This example was given to me by a childminder. I have also heard other examples from nurseries where young boys or girls struggled to make sense of the give-and-take of play with other children, rather than with adults.

To what extent have you experienced this situation with any children?

From time to time, many young children push or hit other children and overlook their visible distress. It would be unrealistic to expect perfection in terms of pro-social behaviour. However, some children seem to be oblivious to the consequences of their actions, when it is an age-appropriate expectation that they would be more obviously aware.

play partner with other children. When circumstances are not on children's side, then their personal and social development can be delayed, along with their language and thinking skills. Children whose early experiences have left them vulnerable can be struggling with some, or all, of the following.

- Doubts about themselves as worthy of other people's attention or affection. Without this secure personal foundation, young children will not manage the skills of friendly contact with other children.

- Use of physical ways of making contact beyond very early childhood, so that these children's attempts to 'make friends' may be experienced literally as pushy by their peers.

- Children are hampered by their limited skills of communication for child-level conversational exchanges, simple question and answer and being able to offer the simple give-and-take of social interaction shown in the example on page 9 of two under-threes.

- When familiar adults have not provided a positive model of emotional literacy, children may be baffled about feelings. They will be far less able to voice their own feelings and preferences in normal three- or four-year-old style.

Over early childhood it is sometimes less than straightforward to assess whether problems can be largely explained by children's unfavourable experiences, or whether some kind of disability is affecting their social development. Learning disabilities may create a situation in which children's behaviour and level of understanding is more like that of a younger child. Disabilities that affect communication are likely to have an impact on a child's social relationships. (Read more about disability on page 35.) Whatever the reason, young children who struggle with the social skills of interaction and communication in play, shine a spotlight on how much has been learned by their more socially adept peers.

Be alert and notice what is working well without your help, as well as those children who – probably without intention – disrupt ongoing play. Who are the young girls and boys that use different positive strategies to join existing play? Do you see three- and four-year-olds who edge into the play gently? Maybe they make a suggestion in words for the Goldilocks game, or they offer resources as their strategy to become more active in the castle building project. These children do not simply barge into a game: physically or trying to seize the lead in words. Nor do they call on an adult as their first or only option.

Young children equally need to find ways to leave a game or play companion. Sometimes it works simply to wander away from the castle.

However, sometimes they need adult support that "Ujala says she's had enough of playing Goldilocks for now".

Enabling social interaction between young children

There is a strong focus in guidance around the UK about the importance of personal and social development.

Such written materials are often less clear about how to create the favourable circumstances for children to make the social contacts which can lead to sustained friendships. The good news is that many aspects of what is regarded as best practice in early years provision work very well to support children's social interaction in a developmentally appropriate way. The main issues are a welcoming learning environment and well-informed, emotionally warm practitioners who understand the difference that their behaviour makes for young children's learning.

An environment for easy social contact

Early years practitioners have been given practical guidance and plenty of encouragement to look closely at the physical environment in which babies and children spend their days.

Thoughtful teams and childminders make the most of possibilities to create smaller, comfortable spaces, as well as more open areas and consideration for children's through routes indoors and outside.

Look closer: the importance of pleasant bathrooms

The design of Oakfield Nursery School included a lot of thought about the bathrooms. Young children spend a lot of time in the bathroom: using the toilet as well as washing their hands before meals and food preparation. The manager and team accept that young children also socialise in the bathroom, enjoying the company of another child during this practical task and having a chat with each other.

The bathrooms have been designed to have as much natural light as possible and to have taps and soap dispensers that are easy for older toddlers and young children to operate independently. The team at Oakfield ensure that children are safe and have learned to manage their own care. However, they have also recognised that bathrooms deserve attention, because they are part of the social environment for young children.

Space and equipment to suit babies and young toddlers

This attention to space and spaces starts with the environment for babies and young toddlers. In the settings mentioned in the examples, the whole team was confident to use the physical learning environment to the full. Careful attention was paid to the whereabouts of babies and toddlers, or any older child who needed more support. But the team leaders had ensured that practitioners did not feel every child had to be in full sight all the time. The environment was safe and had secure outer boundaries. So, even babies and toddlers could enjoy little spaces that felt hidden to them. The slightly older children moved confidently around their indoor and outdoor environment, relishing the temporary and more permanent structures in which they could play in some privacy.

Look closer: a social environment to support babies

In Little Learners Nursery School, the home base room for babies up to about 12 months is The Baby Nest. Once young toddlers are stable walkers they move into The Snug. The physical environment of The Baby Nest has been organised so that babies can access materials easily. The choices made over furniture and resources also mean that babies and young toddlers can easily play alongside each other. They can access the same materials, but with space and sufficient resources for each baby to have enough for themselves.

The Baby Nest (like every room in Little Learners) has a cosy corner, attractively organised with cushions and drapery. It is easy for a baby or toddler to settle comfortably in this corner and watch what is going on in the room. It is equally easy for two older babies or young toddlers to spend time here together, with or without an adult.

Until I spent time in The Baby Nest, I had never thought about the height of tables that are designed for use with young children. Most tables are designed to be appropriate for children sitting in a small chair. However, older babies leaning on a table for support, or choosing to sit on the floor, can find a standard nursery table higher than ideal to get involved in an activity on the surface of

the table. The Baby Nest has tables with shorter than usual legs. Sometimes resources are placed on the table and babies or young toddlers can approach the resource (like the cornflour activity described on page 19) from each side. Individual babies have space to access materials and can also see clearly what their peers are doing.

A wide range of open-ended resources are provided in baskets, which are easily accessible. Also there is a selection of different sensory boards fixed to the wall at the right height for sitting babies to touch. Each board offers a different experience of materials (securely fixed) that can be touched or manipulated for movement or sound. These kinds of materials are very well suited to little hands and interests. But a further advantage of the design is that babies and toddlers can look easily and see what their companions are doing.

The moulded plastic toys and consoles (that are enthusiastically marketed as suitable for babies) were absent from the nurseries I visited. One problem with these materials is that they do not offer easy scope for babies to play companionably with each other. Everything is fixed to the same plastic base shape, so it is not possible for babies or toddlers to select an item each. In contrast, a sensory board has separate items, such as bells or other sound makers that can be tapped or twisted. Materials have different textures that babies and children explore by touching or stroking. The further advantage of open baskets, or sensory boards, is that

babies are easily able to watch what another baby or toddler does. Everything is not crowded into such a small space, that observant babies have no choice but to lean well into the play of another baby or toddler. I have seen mobile babies and young toddlers watch carefully as a peer chooses and waves around one item from a collection of plastic bottles, with different materials secured by a tight top. (This is an example of a good reason to use plastic.) Very young observers have sometimes then chosen an item of their own.

Spaces that invite social interaction

Some smaller spaces, often with a den-like element of enclosure, give children a more intimate and private environment. These spaces may be temporary structures, like a sheet over an A-frame or a large cardboard box. Early years settings have increasingly looked at the possibilities of lightweight tents, which can work indoors as well as in the garden. Sometimes there is a more permanent structure like a wooden shed or little house, which is organised by the children themselves.

These small spaces enable children to get together with chosen companions for play, but often also for conversation between children. Some children feel intimidated within a very busy group setting, with no peaceful spaces. They are neither 'quiet' nor 'shy' children; they just do not want to shout and they dislike the noise. Children like to get together in more private spaces but they will often invite an adult to join their social group in the cave made out of cushions or to bend double to enter a wicker structure.

Look closer: constructing child-size spaces

In Little Learners Nursery School, a robust small building occupies one corner of the garden. The shack-sized edifice is large enough for several children to go into and came about as a joint enterprise.

The idea of building their own little house arose from the enthusiasm of one child who came back from a camping trip with his family. The children worked with each other and the adults to research possible building materials and a local builder was asked to visit and give his advice and help. The decision was to build with a range of different materials. So the sturdy little house has straw-type roofing, different kinds of bricks, some corrugated iron, and one section with closely bound sticks, as well as wood for some of the frames.

The children were justifiably proud of their building and keen to show it to me as a visitor. Readers will be able to envisage how much these mainly three- and four-year-olds learned through this first-hand experience – in every aspect of their development.

A suitable physical environment, in which babies and children can move, and also settle down to play, is complemented by enough space for children to play with resources, without being jammed

up against something, or someone else. Thoughtful practitioners aim to have a generous array of resources but to avoid the situation when so much is out that children have trouble playing in such a cluttered environment. In a similar way, practitioners ensure that the day or session feels relaxed, not rushed, and that babies or children are not over-organised to move frequently from one activity, or part of the setting, to another.

In contrast, if practitioners are tempted to pack too much into a day or session, there is a risk that children have restricted time to choose to play or chat together.

Equipment that encourages being together

Even a short browse through catalogues aimed at early childhood shows a huge array of equipment and furniture, along with play resources. Everyone has a budget and it is important to ensure that it is spent on well-made equipment that will tolerate the normal wear and tear of play. The following list highlights key aspects of design, and its impact on young children to consider.

- Does the equipment or furniture enable young children to gather around, while still having enough personal space?

- Can large equipment be used in pretend play?

- Where will items go: indoors or outdoors?

- Can children use all sides of a trolley?

- Can young children, who are not directly involved, stand close enough to watch?

- Is there enough room so that different small groups do not feel their play space has been invaded?

Some resources and games have real potential for supporting play involving two or more children (some examples follow) now. Yet, even very promising resources cannot offer this support in an unpromising learning environment. The settings described in this book all had an atmosphere of relaxed purposefulness. Considerable adult thoughtfulness had created a well-resourced environment. However, it was equally important that babies and children were able to spend sustained amounts of time in activities that clearly absorbed them.

Look closer: equipment suitable for pairs and small groups

Think about how these descriptions include what you already do, and maybe what you could introduce.

In 'The Snug' at Little Learners Nursery School, the eldest children are older twos. A low sand table enables a small number of children to play with this resource at the same time, with enough elbow room for everyone. I watched two children, a boy and a girl on each side of the table, accompanied by a practitioner who was digging with equal enthusiasm. The adult commented on some of the play but not all. The children were able if they wished to watch and copy the adult. But this age group also choose to imitate each other, when they are able to see clearly what a peer is doing. In this case, the girl put her bucket upside down and did a rat-a-tat-tat with her spade on the surface. The boy watched her actions and then copied with his own bucket and spade.

The painting easels are set low and are a double-width design. As I could see during my visit, this makes it very easy for two children to paint alongside each other. Both painters have a generous amount of space but also they are positioned in a way that makes it easy to stop and look at what the other child is doing and comment if they wish.

The generous resources in the base rooms for three- and four-year-olds enable children to select materials and to organise themselves. Children can easily spend time on their own, if they wish. But the layout also welcomes small groups of play companions to get together.

A deliberate decision was taken, when the Pre-School Room was equipped with a computer, to have a seat wide enough for two children to sit together. Consequently, they can work cooperatively on some programmes. The nursery installed an interactive whiteboard fixed to one wall and the advantage of this resource is that children can choose to create together. They have the space to make large mark-making movements in a joint, chosen enterprise.

· ·

In Oakfield Nursery School, children could access drawing and painting outside in the garden but there were also indoor opportunities. A group of three- and four-year–olds were busy at one point in a room dedicated to art and craft. Children were able to access this room through the day. The resources were set up so that two or three children could gather around the separate tables or wheeled trolleys with soft sand, wax sand (which can be moulded) and water. This organisation meant that they had enough space and items in each resource area that play could be sustained without waiting for items or space to operate.

I noticed how the children had the scope to look and listen to each other, chat and play. They were also keen to show me how the wax sand worked – I was unfamiliar with this resource. Two girls at the water trolleys chose often to work together on filling enterprises that needed one child to hold a large bottle with a funnel and the other to do the pouring.

At the same time, three other girls were busy in the area just outside this room. This small space is equipped with a small table, chairs and mirrors. The girls were engaged in a child-initiated imaginative sequence around drafting and posting letters. Their sustained play lasted for most of the time that other children were busy inside the room (well over half an hour).

· ·

On the day of my visit to Red Hen Day Nursery, I watched many examples of children choosing to play together. For instance, a dolls' house with an open design enabled a mix of fours and older (some children from the small school holiday group) to play together in the round. They were able to access the rooms of the house and organised the available furniture from the different sides.

In another room, a large, low black builder tray enabled a few children to play together with the same materials. Three boys (five- and six-year-olds) from the holiday group were working together with items that could be made into a boat. They had paper instructions which they consulted as they decided what and how to build. Two of the boys were especially interested in watching the third boy, who seemed to be the most enthusiastic builder of the group.

Supporting Children's Social Development

Resources like floor dominos or simple card and board games enable older threes and fours to get together with materials of a size that everyone can see. At this age, children are most likely to need and welcome an adult as co-player. With this kind of shared experience, older fours and fives may then be able to organise their own game. Over the years, I have observed many instances of under-fives, in some cases under fours, keen to be involved in a board or card game with co-players and basic rules. This time, I watched in Little Learners Pre-School Room as one practitioner worked alongside two children who wanted to set up a large floor puzzle which created a board game. This adult was sharing her attention between these two children and a third child sitting close who was playing with a set of stacking blocks. The child had built the stack and now took turns with the adults in a game that required partners to alternate in removing single blocks, without the whole edifice collapsing.

In all the settings I visited, adults were friendly and easily available play partners, but did not in any way intrude on play where children were entirely happy organising themselves. Consequently, the few adult-organised playful events –like the parachute play examples below – were a refreshing change of pace for the children, and absolutely not yet another adult-led activity in a long list throughout the day. It was also significant that the children only spent a small proportion of their day in group games or events. Children had spent the majority of their day in social interactions they had chosen. So, again a focused game, in which everyone had a part to play, was a refreshing change for them.

Look closer: enjoying parachute play

During my day in Red Hen Day Nursery, I watched two versions of parachute play. During the morning, the school holiday group of eight children (five- to seven-year-olds) came out into the grassy area known as 'The Mound' with Mike, the practitioner responsible for this group. They had a lively time with a large parachute. Part of their play was a series of parachute games, which require for everyone to take their part in holding the material, heaving it up and down or being the person who this time goes underneath.

The boys and girls also had some energetic run-and-chase games involving the parachute. These older children were careful to keep safe space between them and the babies and toddlers, who were also in this large outdoor space with their practitioners. But these very young children were highly entertained by the spectacle of the older children. They watched with great interest as the older children disappeared behind the mound and reappeared at speed, the parachute flapping behind them.

Later in the day, I watched a group of two-year-olds enjoying a large stretch of red lycra material, sitting indoors in a circle on the floor. These very young children cooperated well as they sat and worked the material up and down from their seated position. There was a lot of happy giggling as individual children took turns to wriggle under the material or hide under it and be 'found'.

· ·

Towards the end of the afternoon in Little Learners Nursery School, I joined a circle of eight children (older twos and threes) and four other adults. A large stretch of red lycra material was held by everyone and it worked like an indoor parachute for little hands. We all sat in a circle and these two- and three-year-olds were able to take part enthusiastically in a shared playful enterprise that depended on everyone working together. The adults kept the activity simple enough for this age group, yet it was lively and held all the children's attention.

They had five soft toys placed on the lycra: four fairies with different features that the children could distinguish and a wizard. The children worked with the adults to bounce these toys really high, with the result that the figures soon bounced off. The interest and lively conversation was about how high it was possible to bounce the fairies and the wizard, which ones had bounced right off the parachute, and where were they now?

The children were very keen on this joint activity. They were happy to sit in a circle for something physically lively. Also, this activity was planned for towards the end of a day in which the children had spent a considerable amount of time outdoors from choice. They were ready to sit a while.

Best practice with and for young children is to plan flexibly around meaningful routines. A positive approach to the flow of a session, a day and the changes over a week supports children's sense of wellbeing. Along with a welcoming physical environment, and emotional warmth from the adults, a sense of 'I know what's happening' helps young children to feel physically at ease and emotionally secure.

In my visits to many nurseries, I have seen the positive consequences for children when teams and individual practitioners had considered how they managed time and the timing of events. The adults did not forget that early childhood lasts for years; there is no need to push many changes of activity into a narrow band of time. Equally, these practitioners paid close attention to the transition times. They had considered how best to manage the beginning and end of each day. They had also thought about when young children were part of meal times or the group of children took their time to relocate to other parts of the nursery – indoors or outside.

Young children like an understandable pattern to their day; predictable routines matter and they enable young boys and girls to be active working members of a home-like nursery community, or your home as a childminder. The same advantages apply in children's own family homes, when parents take this positive outlook on domestic routines. Of course, adult-dominated routines do children no favours. They are likely to feel harassed by rigid timing that interrupts their play and gives them little, if any, time to volunteer for 'jobs'. I have heard children use this exact word in a wholly positive way as they choose to wash up the paint pots or get busy with laying the table.

Social learning and domestic routine

Children gain socially from being part of tidy-up time and they learn practical life skills – not least that it is not alright to leave trails that somebody else will always put straight. Involvement in routines and practical domestic tasks (like the example about food preparation on page 25) offer a meaningful context for children to learn patterns of social behaviour. They bring alive taking care of shared possessions or the physical environment enjoyed by this small community: your nursery, or home as a childminder.

I have visited many early years settings who take this positive approach to social learning. Tidying up is a valued routine within the day or session, so it is given sufficient time. Children have a warning, sometimes a recognised sound like a little bell, that it will be time to tidy up within a few minutes. There is often the general assumption that children will work on tidying up the resources where they are playing, when it time to make space for lunch or a half-day session is coming to the close. I have also observed situations in which young children have appreciated a short conversation about which area or set of resources they would like to tackle with their play companions. Even the eldest children in nurseries are still very young, so wise practitioners move around, working with the children and encouraging their involvement. Guidance is offered when necessary: "Do you remember where we keep..?", "Can you see anything else that needs tidying up..?" or "I can see…" and an indication of an area or item that has been missed.

A gentle pace for ordinary routines gives young children a chance to make decisions. Some of these options will be about their companions: if we go in pairs on a walk to the park, whose hand do I choose to hold? When we are tidying up, do I have time to organise how me and my friends want to tackle the mess that is currently the book corner? I have observed many tidy-up times where even the youngest want to be part of the routine because it is a shared, social event. They find their involvement a source of personal satisfaction: a more useful concept for adults to bear in mind than the insistence that everything must always be 'fun'. A well-organised physical environment helps, because children working together know how to put specific resources back in their right place, so they

can easily be found next time. I have watched as considerate adults often encourage children with 'well done', offer help with: "Do you know where that goes?" and thank a child who has showed a peer where or how to store this resource.

Thoughtful early years teams all take snack and lunch times seriously as social occasions, as well as the time when everyone gets on with the important business of eating and drinking. Lunchtime will be the same for all children, although babies or very young toddlers may still follow their personal routine, not yet aligned with the slightly older children. Snack time can be run in a flexible way and the adult decision about a rolling snack, or a fixed time, should depend on observation to judge what works best for the children.

Many settings now run a flexible snack time, although I have known some who responded to children's clearly expressed preference that they liked to sit down all together. The consistent message for best practice is to watch and listen: is the current system working well from the children's perspective? Different routines can ensure a social time and meet the adult responsibility to ensure young children develop healthy habits of eating and drinking.

Look closer: routines as regular social events

Little Learners Nursery School offers an attractive environment for snack and meal times, which run in a slightly different pattern, according to the age group,

I sat with the two-year-olds in 'The Snug' for their snack time. The small tables offer a small group atmosphere, with no more than four or five young children sitting with an adult. Each table has a vase with real flowers – none of which got knocked over. The atmosphere was peaceful and conversational.

These young children were able to help in handing out individual plates and passing around plates with fruit and other snacks. Again, the practitioners in this room were ready to ease the social interaction between children in a friendly way. They used personal names as part of the conversational flow. Sometimes this was within a "Well done" to a child who had accepted the task of handing out the plates. But they also used children's names to bring children's attention to what a young child was trying to indicate, for instance: "Johnny would like some grapes".

The snack for the slightly older children is available throughout the morning, and the same in the afternoon, set out on tables on a covered platform, to one side of the outdoor area. Children access their drink and fruit, when they want and with the companions they choose. They can use cutting boards and knives if they want to cut up their fruit.

Guiding social interaction

Young children are capable of learning patterns of pro-social behaviour. They are potentially able to cope with the social skills which ease small group interaction. Yet, it is essential to recall that such behaviour is learned from experience over early childhood. The ability to take turns does not put down strong roots just because grown-ups say. "You ought to take your turn". The genuine willingness of young children to put their head to one side – as they often do – and listen to what another child wants to say does not appear just because a certain birthday has come and gone. A significant amount depends on the behaviour of familiar adults: both the direct suggestions and friendly guidance and that adults set a good and visible example of how to behave in socially sensitive ways.

Adults set a good example

Young children, who have experienced respect and courtesy for what they want to say or show, are more likely to take on a habit of listening to others. Adults need to hold realistic expectations, informed by their knowledge of child development. For instance, young children are not necessarily being 'rude' when they 'interrupt'. They literally cannot hold on to a really interesting thought for very long before having to voice it out loud – or lose it.

With appropriate adult support, young children are able to learn social skills, like making space on the sofa for another child or showing they want to say something, without interrupting someone else in full flow in a conversation. These skills can be applied in a broad range of social situations. If you watch children somewhere like a nursery, simple habits of courtesy are used between children, because that is 'what we do here', and not limited to children who are close companions.

Young children do not develop pro-social habits of behaviour because they are told regularly to "be nice" or "you ought to share". Boys and girls imitate what they see and hear; they follow the lead of familiar adults, or older children. They copy saying "can I have..?" rather than grabbing something. Even young children recycle the friendly query like "are you alright?", which they have heard in a tone of voice that communicates caring.

Affirming children's positive learning

Children also learn most powerfully from timely and encouraging affirmation of what they have done: for instance, moving up to give a peer some room to sit in comfort. It is less effective for positive learning when children experience more adult effort going into criticising them for the occasions when children have delayed showing any consideration. Helpful adult behaviour starts with the baby year, along with realistic expectations for what social play looks like in the baby or young toddler version.

Look closer: enabling social play for toddlers

In the Baby Nest of Little Learners Nursery School, three toddlers (aged from 13 to 17 months) were each very engaged in playing with a cornflour mix spread out on a low table. The layout of the table and the adult's close companionship meant that these very young children were able to watch each other and the adult closely; nothing blocked their clear view. The adult's commentary eased the social interaction between babies and young toddlers, who did not yet have the words to talk out loud themselves. So the practitioner commented briefly on what was happening in front of them all: "Sara, would you like some more?" and "Ned's mixing it".

A baby, aged 11 months, chose to join the group and was greeted by the toddlers with: "Hello Janie". The practitioner acknowledged the interest shown by the existing group in the new arrival to the cornflour table with: "Janie's just come in".

The babies and toddlers looked at each other and the adult was alert to the direction of their gaze and commented. For example: "Janie's got the whole bowl" when this baby was handling the bowl in which the cornflour had been mixed. The babies and toddlers all watched closely what the practitioner did with the cornflour. They stared as the runny cornflour mix dripped off her hands onto the table and imitated some of her actions, such as patting the mix on the table. However, she also followed their lead when some babies slapped the cornflour in a different pattern of touch. Overall the practitioner made the difference in creating a happy, playful atmosphere for three, and then four, very young children to play cooperatively with a shared resource in the same space.

The absorbing play with cornflour evolved into an equally enjoyable next phase. These babies and toddlers sat, sometimes two at a time, in a container of warm water. This time was a happy way to wash off the layer of cornflour before they were cuddled in a warm towel and dressed again.

> ### Easing young interactions

Very young children need the friendly presence of familiar adults who create the best circumstances for the earliest friendly contact. However well you know them, you cannot be certain what is in the mind of the baby or toddler who makes the approach. But you can use your greater thinking power to allow for likely possibilities, and you can voice the comment that this child cannot yet say in words. You smooth the way for very young social interaction with comments like: "Jessie's interested in the teddy" or "Liam wants to say 'can I post some bricks too?'". Very young children understand more than they can say themselves. So, there is a good chance that their facial expression will confirm your guess, or that their puzzled look says you have got hold of the wrong end of the stick.

Occasionally, Liam wants the whole posting box; his action is more of a toy raid than a social request. Helpful adults – practitioners and parents alike

– need to be close enough that it is possible to ease the interaction, when young social skills are stretched too far. Practitioners need to be fully comfortable with touch, because sometimes you need gently to intervene. This behaviour is not 'a physical intervention' in the same way as if you use your physical strength wisely in order to split up two fighting five-year-olds.

Look closer: supporting social interaction between very young children

In Little Learners, toddlers move into The Snug when they are stable walkers and stay here until they are between two and two-and-a-half years of age. A great deal of care is taken over this internal transition, and with children's other moves between home base rooms over the years. Time is taken to enable a child to become familiar with their new key person, and the other adults in the room. But the team is also very aware that children new to a room need support to get to know other children. If possible, they move with a peer from their previous room, but there is still an array of unfamiliar faces.

On the day of my visit I was able to see practitioners easing the social interaction in ways that were appropriate for these slightly older, but still very young children. For instance, each child has their own home photo book that they can access easily. I watched as one child and a practitioner enjoyed looking at the child's book together. The adult was naming people in the photo and commenting. But this young child

was able – in contrast with the toddlers in the example on page 30 – to add her own comments as well.

Later in the morning, a practitioner and two girls were looking at the photo book that belonged to one of the children, Sophie. The other child was very interested and asked questions about who was in the photos. After a short while, a third girl called Ruby brought across a tin of resources and joined the small group. The two children were interested in this new resource and watched as the adult tried out the clicking of the sound makers in the tin. After watching carefully, Sophie opted to try some of the sound makers as well.

Opportunities for children to direct themselves

During my visits to many early years settings I have noticed the extent to which emotionally secure young children are able to organise themselves. Small groups form and sometimes re-form, within a well-resourced and free flow environment. Confident children, certainly as young as older twos and young threes, are very able to ask and direct familiar adults, whom they know to be only too happy to behave as an equal play partner. It was easy to see how the children trusted the adults to respect the social rules of play and not highjack a game or pretend play theme for their own adult agenda.

In the settings described in this book, but also in other nurseries I visited (Lindon, 2012a, 2012a, 2011) the practitioners spread out in a natural way throughout the indoor and outdoor environment. Adults were also close enough that children could easily ask for support or strike up a conversation. Sometimes, an adult stayed with a group, being directed by the children or told what was happening – like the example of the water pump on page 31. Adults gravitated to where children were busy, as well as sometimes sitting in peace and watching – when children often gravitated towards the sitting adult. Requests for help with a play resource, or to read a book that an individual child had chosen, often led to an informal, small social group as one or two other children tucked themselves alongside the activity or snuggled up to share the book.

Keep any groups small

A continuing theme for best practice with young children is that they should not be required to spend large amounts of their day or session in large group interaction – especially if that group time is sedentary. Social interaction can be supported by 'groups' when those are informal, self-chosen groups of play companions. The examples on page 17 are a reminder that children can manage, and enjoy a few social interactions and games in groups when the shared activity is lively – physically and mentally. It is unrealistic to expect under-fives to be fully engaged in large group activities in which they have to sit nicely and wait ages to have their say. The unrealistic expectations also extend to what

Food for thought

It is worthwhile reflecting upon what happens to the pattern of communication when a group of adults grows in size. Often, these are the likely developments.

- Once a discussion group of adults grows beyond four people, the pattern of interaction between the group members becomes progressively less equal. Some individuals talk a lot more than others.

- People have to hold their thought and wait for a gap, or else interrupt.

- Quieter members do not speak up and the longer they are silent, the harder it is to start. They daydream, doodle (if possible) and learn the habit of disengaging from this meeting or even a social group.

So, what about young children? Why should we think that they can gain much at all from sitting in a group of over ten other children, sometimes more? What do you think?

children are likely to learn, if the adults believe that lengthy group chat sessions are the best way to promote pro-social behaviour.

Social interaction and pretend play

Young friends play together and by the time they are three and four years of age, they spend a lot of time in pretend play. Ros Garrick et al. (2010) report how three- and four-year-olds become enthused when asked their views on play. In every setting except one (of the 15 in the study) young children spontaneously mentioned pretend play. In several settings, the children talked more about their pretend play than any other kinds of play.

Books about early childhood tend to use phrases like fantasy play, imaginative play and role play. The writers, and early years practitioners who use this choice of words, tend to mean slightly different kinds of play each time. From the children's perspective – and the words they use – it is all about pretend. It does not matter if the pretence is about fantasy characters or creatures, about making a meal with playdough (that this child is definitely not going to eat) or pretending to do adult jobs like that of a postman or doctor.

Pretend play is important to children

The power of pretend play, especially when the adults resist any temptation to over-organise and pre-package the play, is that children explore strong psychological themes out of choice.

Judy Dunn (2004) observed that even under-fives weave in their understanding, and confusions, about why people behave the way they do. She suggests – and I would agree – that self-chosen, child-directed pretend play is an effective forum for young children to extend their social understanding. Vivian Gussin Paley (2004) documented years of pretend play and the making and telling of stories by threes and fours in the nursery. Her accounts of the absorbing interests of young children show how fascinated they are by what people do and why: their motives and intentions.

Both Judy Dunn and Vivian Gussin Paley observed the chosen play of young children: genuinely child-initiated pretend sequences. Paley's descriptive accounts show how children's chosen themes can last for a very long time, yet also how this crucial learning is disrupted in nursery days that are sub-divided by adult plans. Paley also recounts how children really want to talk about the themes in their play and pose the questions that matter to them: about stories or the actions of real play companions in their chosen theme. These discussions were sometimes part of a very flexible small group time in the nursery. However, the content of the discussion was determined by the children and not by an adult's session plan.

The best way forward in supporting children's social development is to ensure that it is easy for children to choose to join in shared enterprises, many of which will be initiated by children and not by one of the adults. Young children practise and fine-tune social skills by having very good reasons to use them (look again at the example of the fire pit on page 10) and with the additional, discreet help from attentive adults.

Look closer: generous time for pretend play
In Red Hen Day Nursery, the team has reflected on how much some children want to bring in favourite toys from home. They respect children's play and have discussed how best to welcome physically very lively games and the issues around pretend themes of goodies and baddies.

Some boys in Red Hen became very enthused about the fictional character Ben10© and one boy in particular was very keen to bring in his Ben10 scooter. The team decided that this should be possible and observed that the scooter was the focus for cooperative play around this pretend theme. The team discussed and set boundaries with the children to ensure that very lively play did not impose on other children and some ground rules about children's own possessions. The general approach was to have a timed period when a child's own toy, like the scooter, was part of general play and then to encourage the child to put the item in a safe place until the end of the day.

During my day in Red Hen Day Nursery, I watched as three boys (aged three and four years) set up and ran a pretend

car wash in the outdoor courtyard. They organised their water supply by filling containers from the nearby water tray and were ready to sponge down the vehicles as other children brought them. The car washing was extended by one child who informed one child driver that "your car needs some petrol". A practitioner was nearby and encouraged children to fill up buckets from another source when the tray was empty. She also reassured a child who had brought in his vehicle for a wash and inadvertently kicked over the bucket of water. The practitioner went with a girl who was watching the play and together they brought back more water. The girl then became part of the washing crew.

During the afternoon, four children and a practitioner were busy for a long stretch of time in sand area of the Kindergarten outdoor area. They were working together with big buckets, ice cube trays, tart tins, pots and pans, wooden spoons and lots of water. The group was interested in putting water and sand into the different containers, mixing everything up then using their various spoons – small and large – to scoop out the mixture and create large wet shapes in the sandy base. One child commented accurately: "It's really gooey".

The play moved into a hunt for buried treasure, with serious discussion between Max and Natalie. Max announced that "it's a treasure" and Natalie wanted confirmation that "I found it first, I did". Then Max wanted to check "did you bury it?" and the conversation carried on about who found it first until the practitioner suggested:"Why don't we see if we can find any more treasure?". There was a brief exchange when Natalie asked: "Can I borrow it?" wanting to use the large white ice cube tray. The practitioner offered the use of a sand timer, if they wanted to organise turns. But in the end the children sorted out turns informally.

Meanwhile, two boys had together created an impressive puddle in the dip in the dry ground. They had used a large container of water to fill up the space. Then they took turns jumping into the puddle. Soon they were joined by a girl and there was a lot of enthusiastic jumping, which removed some of the water. (The children all had Wellington boots and their overalls on).

At the other end of the Kindergarten outdoor space, several children had spent much of the afternoon creating a teahouse with a teddy bears' picnic inside a huge cardboard box turned on its side. By the end of the day two girls had organised an impressive display with the teddy bears, cups and plates laid out for tea and a mixture that was the food. They had made a concoction in a large washing up bowl of teabags, conkers, assorted green stuff and water.

The girls running the teahouse served their guests and carefully spooned out the mixture for the bears and four (real) children who waited patiently to be served their tea. The mixture was spooned out onto plates for the pretend tea and explanations were given that it was sausage rolls, corn, carrots and teabags. The guests were encouraged with: "Would you like a seaside sandwich?", and "you'll love a teabag, Peter".

Normal problems in young social interaction

Judy Dunn (2004) argues that childhood friendships are the forum in which young children learn about empathy and resolving disagreements, because they care so much about what happens with other children who matter to them. Young children will have quarrels, they will fall out temporarily with their friends, but they very much want to sort out those disagreements. Younger children will usually have adults – parents or early years practitioners – relatively near by, close enough to hear the shouts of anger or cries of distress. So, it is important that any adult contribution is genuinely helpful, from the children's perspective. Any adult intervention really has to put friendly contact back on track, rather than just paper over the cracks. Unresolved disagreements will simply re-emerge in play sooner or later.

Disagreement is part of play

Disputes between children are not in themselves negative events. Adults are profoundly unhelpful, if they take the line

Food for thought

Children over the generations have had a go at resolving the normal ups and downs within friendships. Reflect on your own childhood – as early as you can accurately recall.

- What led to disagreements, even outright argument, between you and your childhood friends?

- Did you usually sort it out without adult intervention? If so, what strategies do you now realise you and your friend used?

- Can you recall adults who offered to help? What suggestions were actually helpful to you and your friends?

Links to your practice

What decides you to intervene in a dispute between two or more children? How do you judge when they need your help?

Here are some ideas to think about and discuss with your colleagues.

- The dispute has been going on for some time, or is an argument that has simmered on and off all day.

- One child seems less able to make their point than the other(s).

- The volume of communication is increasing.

- At least one child in the dispute looks or sounds distressed.

- The dispute has turned physical, with pushing or hitting.

that there are to be no disagreements or raised voices here. Within normal, lively play, some disputes between children are part of social interaction, and the whole process of learning to get along together. Occasional shouts and – yes the shoves too – are not a sign of serious maladjustment. It is a different situation if you observe a pattern in which children cannot learn to regulate their behaviour over time and with your active help.

Responsible practitioners and parents give a consistent message that "here we don't sort things out by shoving each other" and they show as well as say: "We use our words". Falling out is just as much part of young social interaction as those occasions when young children warm your heart by their active consideration of another's child feelings. Both patterns are within perfectly normal child behaviour and it is not unusual that an example of each happens within less than five minutes between the same two children.

The HighScope approach, described by Betsy Evans (2002), focuses on how practitioners can help with social conflict at the time that children (over-threes) have a dispute. The approach is designed to model to children how the skills work, so that in time they can resolve arguments themselves. The adult takes the role of mediator, rather than trying to solve any problem for children, or telling them what to do. A familiar adult invites children with: "What happened?", rather than the adult deciding who is in the wrong or who had it first (which you rarely know for certain). The adult helps young children to listen to each other and to talk about "what could we do about this problem?". The adult helps them to decide what would be best, and offers possible ideas, if the children are stuck. Support is available for children to put their idea into practice. With this guidance, even four-year-olds become more able to talk about disagreements with peers.

Undoubtedly, it will be easier for you to help when children have learned to be confident that familiar adults will listen properly to what has happened. Even young children will give some ground on a dispute when experience tells them that adults are open-minded. Children also need to feel reassured that adults will let an issue go once it has been resolved – rather than hark back to the dispute for ages. In a warm, and forgiving, emotional environment, children are more likely to say sorry and mean that word, or show their genuine regret by wanting to 'make things better' for another child.

When conflict resolution is harder

As was discussed on page 11, some issues can complicate this social learning for young children. Disabilities which affect social development and communication may mean that some children are behaving like a younger child, or that they will always be puzzled by the social subtleties that their peers understand. The challenge for supportive adults is to balance the needs of all the children.

- It is appropriate for you to make allowance for children who struggle to learn the social and conflict resolution skills that their potential play companions have grasped, at least partly. However, you are responsible for implementing a realistic plan to help children when usual methods of support are not working.

- You can help children to understand why a few of their peers do not understand that, of course, you should ask rather than barge into play. Young children can be supportive of peers who, for whatever reason, find it very hard to do the right thing. They can accept that Jason absolutely has to hold onto his cars or anything else with wheels, and does not want anyone else to play.

- However, adults need to keep a close eye on how often young children are expected to be flexible over the usual ground rules of play, or to tolerate what they feel to be inconsiderate behaviour from a peer.

- It should largely be up to the adults to ensure that inclusion works and that no child is excluded for want of careful adult supervision. Other children get irritated if the adult reaction to Kayleigh's throwing everything is that yet more resources have been removed from the environment for everyone.

Best practice for supporting social development

This section will explore the role of the manager and other members of the senior team to guide and advise early years practitioners. Some issues, from other parts of the book, are revisited here. The aim is to consider the positive impact of choices that practitioners, and entire teams, make. Best practice with young children is reflective: thinking about what you do and why, recognising the choices you make and checking assumptions.

Positive relationships within a small community

Over most of the 20th century, the majority of children younger than the age for statutory education, developed socially within the boundaries of their own extended family and immediate neighbourhood. Within the last couple of decades of the century it became ever more common that children experienced some kind of early years group provision before they entered primary school.

Young children really seem to enjoy their time in nursery when the emotional and physical environment is appropriate for their age and needs. The Effective Provision of Pre-School Education research programme (http://eppe.ioe.ac.uk/eppe/eppeintro.htm) has now followed a large number of young children into their secondary school years. The study found that good quality early years provision offered benefits in terms of some aspects of social development. Young children's social adjustment was assessed by a familiar early years practitioner and the research was mostly interested in patterns of pro- or anti-social behaviour, relevant to children's ability to cope in primary school. These are important issues for child development, but are less central to the immediate social world of children themselves.

Being able to listen in a group, the ability to focus on a given task, age-appropriate independence and understanding ground rules for behaviour, all make life considerably easier within the specialised environment of a primary school classroom (Lindon, 2012d). However, young children need to develop the social sensitivity that enables warm personal relationships, including close friendships. Some of the associated social skills will also be advantageous for interaction in the classroom. However, the social courtesies of large group life, led by an adult, are not the same as the intimacy of friendship. So, although frameworks like the Early Years Foundation Stage tend to emphasise the group social skills, these are only part of social learning for children.

Home-like early years provision

Time in nursery, pre-school or playgroup is so usual now, that there is sometimes the implication that children cannot develop socially without this experience. Yet, a significant proportion of the adult population in the UK developed successfully as social beings while spending their early childhood at home. We – this group includes myself – were not socially bereft; we made friends, and decided whom we did not like. We learned the social rules of give-and-take in a child's world and resolved disputes – or failed to do so – within the physical boundaries of our family home and immediate neighbourhood.

The message of this reminder is that young children need a homely environment wherever they spend their days. They have not started 'school' and they are not 'pupils'. Their social development should not be viewed exclusively through the lense of 'school readiness'.

Look closer: Feeling part of a small community

The owners of Red Hen Day Nursery have always aimed for a home-from-home feel to the environment and the flow of each day. The consequence is that children are able to be part of a wide range of shared events, not all of which would be classified as 'play'. It is a reminder that children's social awareness grows through different kinds of experiences and feeling a valued part of a small community.

Meals and cooking

The nursery kitchen is an ingenious design, which combines appropriate safety in terms of a working kitchen, with easy access for the children. The kitchen is open to the nursery by means of a substantial hatch area and worktop. On the children's side they can step up to the wide worktop to see what is happening in the kitchen and chat with the cook. She prepares food on her side of the worktop, so it is easy for children to watch as she makes puddings or food for teatime. Children who are the snack and lunchtime helpers are able to lift down plates or bowls from the worktop or tidy crockery back up.

Children engage in some kind of cooking or food preparation each day. They can chose to be busy directly on the work top or work on nearby tables and then place their bread or cakes onto the worktop

when they are ready for the cook to place in the oven. The organisation of this physical environment enables children to work together or alongside each other in small groups, which encourages opportunities for conversation. The children at Red Hen have a sound understanding about the sources of their food. They see fruit and vegetables growing on the farm where the nursery is based. They understand that meat comes from the animals they see and, the team say that children are matter-of-fact about this knowledge.

On the day of my visit, the school holiday group (five- to seven-year-olds) were busy with Mike (practitioner) preparing apples for the lunchtime pudding. The children peeled and chopped and the conversation flowed as they worked. There was some discussion about the importance of peeling apples, as one of the eldest boys said: "The little people aren't good with peel". Mike was ready to help with the technique for peeling and chopping, demonstrating how if necessary.

. . . .

The day the drains blocked

The team at Red Hen has a strong focus on first-hand experiences for children and making the most of unexpected events within any day. They document the story of each day's events with photos in an album. Children and parents enjoy looking back at this personal record.

The team showed me the story of the day the drains blocked up completely. Photos and a written explanation help recall how one morning the toilets would no longer flush. It became clear that the system was blocked up because somebody – or several somebodies – had been flushing the green paper towels down the toilets, when it should only have been toilet paper.

The children were involved safely in the necessary remedial action. They were fascinated to watch as the drain cover was lifted and the tough (adult) job began of removing the blockage in the outdoor drains. It was an authentic experience for children to understand why the consistent message had always been not to put paper towels down the toilet. Once the drains looked clear, the children were involved in flushing toilets and checking that the water was now running freely along the drain. Then the cover was replaced safely. The children talked about this exciting event for a long time afterwards.

Protecting time for friendships

Early years practitioners often promote the importance of out-of-home experiences for children's learning of a broad range of social skills. In consultations with young boys and girls about what they value about nursery or playgroup, the children themselves often express their enjoyment at being with friends and playing together (Garrick et al., 2010; Williams, 2010). However, some young children experience several changes within early childhood in terms of their attendance at early years provision. Even if these transitions are managed as well as possible by the adults, this sequence is likely to disrupt friendships. Certainly, it seems best for the children if they can experience continuity.

What does flexible provision mean for children?

The manager and senior team in a group setting – or a sole practitioner in the childminding service – need to recognise and deal with circumstances that are likely to disrupt children's social development. Young children need time and regular contact to make the friendly relationships, which can lead to actual friendship.

The challenge for managers in the early years sector is that they are required to offer high standards for early learning, yet also to make places flexible to the needs of working parents. Official pronouncements – from the previous Labour government as well as the Coalition from 2010 – combine promoting the benefits of 'early education' with requiring very flexible 'childcare'. These (pretty much) incompatible demands are not made of the school system. In fact, once children are older and become school pupils, the same flexibility is unwelcome and called 'irregular attendance'.

I have never read any official pronouncement, or national early years guidance, which has openly considered what high flexibility of attendance may mean to the children themselves. On the other hand, I have encountered concerned managers, and their settings' policies, who have made a serious effort to reconcile what may suit parents with proper consideration of the likely impact on children's social network. Flexibility to suit the variable working hours of different parents using the same group provision can well mean unpredictability for young children.

Look closer: time for sustained friendships

Most of the children at Oakfield Nursery School are fortunate in having an uninterrupted home-from-home life in the nursery, usually from the months of being an older baby or young toddler. They become familiar with their own base room and key person, but the larger Oakfield environment also steadily makes sense to them. Their personal portfolios are usually started in the baby room and then expand over the years before children leave for reception class. Each section of a child's time with Oakfield starts with a photo of their key person and a short professional biography of that practitioner.

The great advantage, for children and their family, is that they do not have to negotiate changes between early years provision within early childhood. Close relationships between children are not disrupted. Additionally, like other nurseries I have visited, the manager of Oakfield

has made a considered decision about how much flexibility in attendance is appropriate, if you truly place young children at the heart of your practice.

A consultation project by the Early Childhood Unit (Williams, 2010) put children's views at the centre. The project team wanted to explore three- and four-year-olds' experiences as their part-time (free) early education (for England) place extended from 12.5 hours per week to 15. The key points highlight that practitioners and parents need to think about adjustments that will help young children.

- The children's view was that their main reason for coming to nursery was to be somewhere they were happy and could play. They used play to ease their own transition into a day or session. So children were less at ease when their preferred way of settling was postponed by having to sit quietly for a process like registration. They were not keen about having to sit and wait, doing nothing, before they were collected by a family member at the end of a session.

- Conversation with and observation of three- and four-year-olds from 10 settings showed that the children were often unclear about their daily schedule – summed up by the report's title of, 'Am I staying for lunch today?'. Children valued meal (and snack times) and they looked to practitioners for reassurance when confusion reigned as to who was going home and who was staying.

Links to your practice

It is well worth keeping alert to how children discuss friendship in their spontaneous comments. I picked up two examples in my one-day visits.

The Red Hen Day Nursery (page 26) holiday group, in the earlier example about food preparation, enjoyed long conversations as they worked, including one about friendships. These boys and girls had a lengthy, completely child-initiated discussion about who was friends with whom – not only within Red Hen. The underlying message was clear that friendship was an important topic – worth talking about and worth being clear about the details of the friendship network. There was no indication that non-friends, who were mentioned, were disliked. They just did not have the special status of being a friend.

In Little Learners Nursery School, I sat listening to a small group in the Pre-School Room as they chatted with an adult about what they had done over the morning. The children were keen to talk about their activity, for instance one girl had made a (real) birthday cake. It was noticeable also that children spontaneously recalled who they had been playing with, together with what they had done. The play companions were an important part of how children wanted to talk about their recent play.

Am I staying for lunch today?

■ The project team observed that, on arrival, these young children actively searched the room for familiar faces. Children new to the setting were distressed when children they judged to be their friends were absent. Familiar faces helped all the children to look more secure.

■ These young children were observed to help each other to settle and to comfort peers when they were tired or upset. It is a positive sign that children are sensitive to each other's emotional state. Yet, this social support seemed to be needed – at least sometimes – because of the unpredictability of social interaction for the children.

Friendships across the age range

The study by Ros Garrick et al. (2010) confirmed the importance of having friends in nursery and reception class. Children spontaneously mentioned that it was sad when you had nobody to play with and you did not want to play on your own. Children in this study also wanted to talk about close relationships with children who were not age peers. Children in the full-age-range day nurseries talked with enthusiasm about time spent with much younger children. This affection was often tinged with a sense of confidence from the older child

Links to your practice

Think about what you already do to help children feel at ease. What else should you and your team consider? Here are some thoughts to start the process.

■ In what ways do your team help children to recognise 'who is here today', as well as to anticipate, 'who is going to be here tomorrow?'. Over-threes are able to make much more sense of photos of other children and are also beginning to get a grip on the days of the week.

■ How do you support individual children, in partnership with parents, to understand their own daily schedules? Is there a limit to what adults should ask of young children?

■ How do you ease the entry and exit of children? What makes these important transition times easier for the children (rather than convenient for the adults)?

■ Have you thought about group times from the perspective of children who stay a full, rather than a part day?

During a workshop about transition times, I was given the example of a setting who listened to the objection voiced by the full-day children to having to sit through a 'hello' and 'goodbye' routine twice a day. The practitioners agreed that these three- and four-year-olds could get on with what they wanted in the middle of the day, which was to help organise for lunch. They were capable of waving goodbye to morning friends and informally greeting afternoon ones.

about what they could now manage. Friendships were formed with older children and this possibility was an attraction for some children whose day included an after-school club. Some children were dejected by their loss of older friends, who had moved on from the current setting.

Different ages will mix within the home of a childminder. However, many settings have looked at how to organise provision in ways that enable contact across the age ranges. Babies and children can still have a base room, yet have times of the day when they meet outdoors or they go visiting with an adult to see other rooms in a nursery or centre. Some settings I have visited made good use of times of the day when there were low numbers to bring the ages together – to the obvious pleasure of both older and younger children.

Look closer: choice for play across different ages

There are easy opportunities for children of different ages to mix during the day at Red Hen Day Nursery. Young children learn a great deal through the company of their age peers and adults who are playful companions. But

children also benefit from the company of children who are younger or older than themselves. The older ones can be very caring towards younger children. The younger ones watch and learn from slightly older children, who are now able to play in ways that are qualitatively different from their younger selves.

During the day in the outdoor courtyard area I watched as some older children joined the babies and young toddlers in their dedicated outdoor area across one corner of the courtyard. The slightly older, but still young children (threes and fours) understood about being careful in the babies' garden. They moved with care and were genuinely interested in what the babies were doing. The practitioners responsible for this youngest group were always aware of the babies and an adult was with the outdoor group at the same time. The youngest children were able to pull themselves up by the secure fence and look into the rest of the garden. They were keen to communicate with the slightly older children on the other side and there was a certain amount of passing toys to and fro.

Some slightly older children (up to seven-years-old) were part of the nursery on the day of my visit, since it was the school holidays. These children had attended Red Hen when they were younger and formed a small sub-group, with their own practitioner, Mike. They spent some of the day together and other times in a social mix with the younger children.

At one point in the courtyard garden an adult was playing ball with two children (two and three years of age). These young children were able to take turns in throwing the ball towards the adult, or trying to catch one thrown towards them. There was lot of chortling. But it was also possible slightly later that day for a couple of four-year-olds to have a go at something a bit more challenging. They were welcome to join the holiday group who were playing a game of catch in the courtyard garden. This game was more of a stretch for younger children, since the rule was you sat down as soon you dropped a catch. Mike was part of the game and used his skills to ensure that younger or less adept children had a chance of catching the football.

Adults as social and play partners

Thoughtful adults make a significant difference to the social development of young children. Part of that contribution is creating a positive environment for easy, personal social contact

and managing time to be on children's side. The other important contribution is how adults behave in helping social interaction. Managers, and the senior team, need to ensure that practitioners understand how to behave as a companionable adult: someone who makes close, personal relationships with individual babies and children and who is a friendly partner in communication and play.

> Supporting babies and toddlers

Part of social interaction is learning how to make personal contact and an important part of engaging with another individual is to know and use their name. Of course, young babies are also in the process of understanding that they have a personal name, and learning to respond to that familiar word. Partnership with parents means that the key person for individual babies or children should always have found out whether they are known by shortened version of their name and how to pronounce a name that is unfamiliar to the adult.

Look closer: using names to ease social contact

In Little Learners Nursery School, the practitioners in The Baby Nest took natural opportunities to enable the babies to hear the names of other babies and of the familiar adults who formed the room team. I watched as one practitioner spent time with two babies: Sara who was 15 months and Janie, 11 months. They all looked at photos that had a velcro backing strip, so could be put on and off a board. The two babies were very interested to select, hold and stare at the photos. The practitioner looked closely with the babies and she named objects and people in a conversational way.

Sara and Janie were at an age when the practitioner did not expect them to use names. They were also at the early stage of making sense of picture images. However, the practitioner's communication was developmentally appropriate for supporting the babies' social development. She, and her colleague who then joined the small group, made short descriptive comments about what was happening in the photo. But they also commented briefly on how the babies reacted to the photos: what had apparently caught their attention. There were also simple invitations to look for familiar children in the photo with: "Where's...?".

The practitioners in The Baby Nest used many opportunities to use personal names, in referring to themselves as well as the children. This good practice may seem 'obvious' in quality settings, but everyone does not behave in this helpful way. It is also valuable for teams with good habits of communication to recall why their behaviour makes such a positive difference to young children.

Practitioners sometimes voiced out loud what they were personally doing and used their own name, rather than 'I'. This adjustment to normal adult speech is made in

a natural way and is helpful for babies and very young children. These thoughtful adults supported babies and toddlers to become familiar with the adults' names, with timely comments like: "Are you waiting for Wendy?".

They also used the children's own names frequently and appropriately. One practitioner was playing a peek-a-boo game with a delighted baby. As the cloth was placed over the baby, the adult said: "Where's Sara gone?" and the same when her vest was partly over the baby's head.

> Choosing when to be involved

Of course, adults can be supportive play partners, but it is important that practitioners never under-estimate how much older twos and young threes are able to direct and organise their own social interactions. Young children often welcome your presence, they sometimes really need your help – but it is worth noting when and where they do not need you. Open discussion within a team can help to bring these issues to the surface and team or room planning depends upon sharing observations of social interaction between children.

One of the negative consequences of adult over-involvement in the details of play is how this directing behaviour seriously reduces the scope for children to organise themselves (Lindon, 2010a, 2011). Generous time for genuinely child-initiated play and conversation brings with it time for relaxed social interaction. These unforced experiences enable young children to develop age-appropriate social skills and independence. But they also leave time and space for friendships to flourish.

Look closer: joint enterprises and companionable adults

In Red Hen Day Nursery children have considerable choice over what to play and their play companions. It was noticeable that, as well as time with their peers, children were genuinely keen to get involved in play or practical enterprises with a practitioner.

At the beginning of the morning, five children from the school holiday group had chosen to work with Mike, the practitioner who takes responsibility for this small older group. They had a complex threading task to make a grasshopper that was then supposed to be sensitive to light. The construction was not easy and they persevered through several wrong choices in how they put the grasshopper together. They then talked about how to test its sensitivity to light. One girl fetched a torch but the grasshopper did not respond. They group tried several re-builds of the grasshopper and then decided perhaps it needed natural light and took it outside.

At one point in the afternoon, several children (threes and fours) responded to Alice's invitation to help her set up a large mosquito net canopy. This task needed cooperative effort and joint working. Two children and Alice needed to stand under the netting. They had to hold up the material, while other children fed the poles through the material to create the circular shape that would then enable the net to fall in a way that creates a den. Their hard work paid off and they had their canopy den.

. . . .

In Little Learners Nursery School a small group of three- and four-year-olds, mainly boys, spent much of the morning with intense, cooperative play. They were working in a permanent area equipped with a water source, channels for the water and a sand surround. They took turns to use the hand-operated water pump and explored the movement of water. The large space enabled them to shift water, work with the sand and talk together as they worked scooping up water from the lower sections. There were friendly requests between children like "fill her up, please".

One practitioner was part of this shared enterprise over the morning and was quick to respond to requests for help such as "can you sort it out for me Linda?". She helped on the few occasions when children needed to resolve turn taking over the pump and some special containers. Linda confirmed at one point that "Josh is in charge of the water". The boy who had asked replied confidently: "After Josh, it's my turn again". Linda was a friendly play partner and got as wet as the boys (everyone was in overalls).

The particular layout around the water pump had been created by one boy, Tim. He had secured a length of tubing so that the hand-pumped water shot out, and could be collected in containers by the other children. The usual pattern was that the pumped water flowed down through various wooden troughs. Linda eased the explanation from Tim who asked her: "Tell Josh what it is". She prompted with "what did you call it?" and Tim remembered "an invention". Linda affirmed with "yes, it's your invention".

The boys became interested in placing a pretend beetle in the tubing and watching how far it would shoot out the other end, depending on the power of the pumping and the flow of water. They experimented with catching the beetle in a bucket. At one point Linda added to the exploration by wondering out loud if the pretend beetle would float or sink and some boys checked what happened.

> Not all about 'play'

The best adult play partners keep children safe, but in ways that do not feel oppressive to young boys and girls. Both Red Hen Day Nursery and Little Learners Nursery School have a strong commitment to offering first-hand experiences to children, which draw on the possibilities in the immediate community. The experiences described in the following examples enabled young children to spend time together, and with adults who were only too pleased to let the children's current interest shape the outing. Diane Rich et al. (2005) stress the importance for children of authentic, first-hand experiences. These regular events in the nurseries that I visited show that it is not only activities within a narrow definition of 'play' that are highly likely to support children's social interaction and cooperation skills.

Look closer: social interaction and first-hand experiences

Out across the fields with Red Hen Day Nursery

The nursery is located on a working farm. Children regularly watch the large farm vehicles moving – from the safety of behind the gate or fence. Every day small groups of children with practitioners visit different parts of the land surrounding the nursery. They are able to spend time in the vegetable garden, visit the paddocks and watch the ponies, chickens and pigs. Depending on the season, children are involved in real events like feeding lambs. The children have been very involved in plans for tree planting and other developments for the outdoors. The wetlands area has two linked ponds. These have a shallow slope and it was judged unnecessary to fence the water. Children learn how to be safe, with practitioners' guidance and they are never in this area without an adult.

A small group of children and two adults take a longer trip every day into the land surrounding Red Hen Day Nursery. They can go in different directions, but the day of my visit we went through the vegetable garden along the line of the fence enclosing the sheep and towards the edge of the ploughed field. The Red Hen team have taken care to show children how to be safe in this open, natural area and all that was needed was simple general reminders. On the day of my visit, the specific information was that nobody should touch the fence around the sheep because it had an electric current running through it.

The children had the time to stand and stare, chat – at one point about the maintenance work that was going on part way along the walk – and to enjoy their own chosen activity. The children spent some time using the possibilities of the ploughed field, which was very dry. They jumped across from one edge to another, tried one- and two-step crossings, experimenting with a single stretching leap. Children took turns or spread out; nobody crashed into anyone. They watched each other's technique and then had another go. The potential of the dry folds of earth was used on the neighbouring field edge as a sub-group of children persevered in the challenging physical task of walking some distance along the top of a ploughed furrow.

The other group were involved in a measuring task: one they had planned from a conversation on the previous day. An adult and children had been speculating about what a length of 30 metres would look like in real life. The question had arisen from a book about cars and racing. They had decided that the expanse of the field should provide the opportunity to use a long tape measure several times over and a child had reminded the adults of the plan that morning. They had obtained a tape measure that was six metres long and together worked out that they would need to use this five times along the edge of the field. The group made their plan, which included having a clear marker for where each length started and finished. The group carefully worked their way along the edge of the field until they had stretched the tape measure five times. They looked back with satisfaction to their very first marker, able to announce 30 metres looked like that.

Full days on the beach in a seaside community

Little Learners Nursery School has a strong commitment to enabling children to gain the many advantages of generous time outdoors. The Beach School is their special development, using the opportunities of being in a seaside town. A small group of children go for a full day once a week with two practitioners, and often also a parent or grandparent from families whose children attend the nursery.

Over time, all the three- and four-year-olds experience their times on the beach. Out of season, the group walks through town to the nearest stretch of beach. However, Skegness is a popular resort town and gets very busy in season. So, the nursery then uses a minibus to drive the group a short distance up the coast to a nature reserve which includes the section of beach where a river enters the sea.

The beach group is no more than six to eight children at a time and they have plenty of scope for relaxed exploration, chatting with each other and the adults and setting off on chosen enterprises within the beach area.

On the day that I joined the beach group, they had earlier trekked out together to the edge of the water when the tide was fully out. They had discovered starfish and a range of bugs. Some of the morning was filled with building bug houses with shells and I was able to see the designs the children had created. By the early afternoon the tide was coming in and interest focused on what was happening in the river. At one point several children were creating a 'pond' close to the waters edge and were very active together in filling their hole with sea water.

The children were still using their nets to dredge the inlet for shells and were busy looking for crabs. They also got intrigued with collecting different kinds and sizes of pebbles and seeing what happened when they threw them into the river. Several children chose to explore the intriguing pattern created when handfuls of gravelly sand and pebbles were hurled into the water.

Children worked alongside and together, watching, talking and sometimes copying. They spent some of the afternoon out of choice sitting on the rug with their books, checking out what they had seen today, with the help of the practitioners. The beach groups are equipped with binoculars, magnifying glasses and bug jars which have breather tubes for the bugs, and some have a magnifying base to the jar. The children were especially interested at one point to identify the bugs they had caught and temporarily housed in their bug jars. The children's experiences on the beach are authentic. Sometimes they do not find much at all, yet recently they had found over 40 starfish during a single beach trip.

Fairness and equality in a child's world

Robust equality practice is an integral part of many practical details of how early years provision should be run (Lindon, 2012b). The manager, with the senior team, is responsible for ensuring inclusive practice over recruitment of staff, the offer of places for children or other services for families and the many aspects of children's daily experiences in any setting. The aim is to establish an active respect for diversity and avoid practices that exclude any families, whether this consequence is intentional or not. The aim in early years provision is also to build positive attitudes within the younger generation.

Reflection and discussion - not assumptions

As a manager, you need to support a team atmosphere that welcomes talking through ways to achieve the aim of equality, because frequently the issues are not straightforward. Not least, attempts to foster equality in the social world of young children will falter without a thorough understanding of young social

relations and the rules that children would like to establish about play. I believe that you can only reach a developmentally appropriate approach to equality by reflection on fairness: a concept that makes sense to children.

One of Vivian Gussin Paley's accounts of life in kindergarten has the thought-provoking title, *You Can't Say You Can't Play* (1992). She homes in on the importance of play companionship to three- and four-year-olds. Her descriptions also show there are different reasons why children may choose not to play with other individuals. Susan Grieshaber and Felicity McArdle (2010) suggest that early years practitioners can be so focused on their own perspective of 'learning through play' that they risk overlooking the real life complexities of relationships within play. The authors also present interesting comments from young children (in nursery or the early years of school) about how adults make the rules for what happens in play, or must not happen.

Grieshaber and McArdle give an example of a small group of girls who cooperated with the practitioner's request to include a child who was hovering on the edge of their Cinderella pretend play. The practitioner observed that this girl remained with the game. However, the end of morning review discussion revealed that the girl had been allocated a meaningless role. Her apparent play companions had learned to respond cooperatively to what the adults wanted. Yet, the consequence for the child was to be included but marginalised.

What is actually happening?

Early years practitioners will not help children on the sidelines of play – certainly for any longer than very short term – unless the adults try to understand what is happening. Unless there is a very good reason to intervene, practitioners should respect the choices that children have made for companions. Adults need to balance their responsibilities.

Links to your practice

Susan Grieshaber and Felicity McArdle present their Cinderella example as something that should make practitioners reflect on their role in play. What do you think? What do you predict might be the responses in your team?

It is important to recall what is likely to bring children together as potential play companions. You could look back at the discussion on page 8 about children's need for time and sustained contact. They need opportunities to discover and create shared interests with other children. However, many comments that children themselves express about play remind adults (who used to be children once) that satisfying play rests also on being able to choose your playmates.

- On the one hand, early years practitioners need to deal constructively, and firmly, with rejection between peers on the basis of a child's group identity. If young children discount any possibility of friendship on the basis of a different family faith, then they will never experience shared interests that span that apparent divide.

- On the other hand, it is irresponsible for adults to conclude that discriminatory attitudes fully explain this child's ejection from play, solely because children differ by a visible marker of group identity. This approach is unreflective and unacceptable adult behaviour, in a similar vein to enthusiasm for labelling very young children as bullies (page 11).

- For instance, has this little group of girls pushed Alex away from the pretend cooking with petals, specifically because he is a boy? Have the girls said something dismissive that supports this possible interpretation? Or, if Alex's key person observes more closely, is he trying to join the play by throwing earth into the mix and not listening to the wails of "don't do that!".

Children with English as an additional language

Children who do not share a common language can be inventive in showing more than telling. They are often welcomed, or succeed in integrating themselves into ongoing play, despite having few, if any, words in common with the other children. However, adults should not underestimate the value for children of being able to talk to each other.

Children who have developed spoken language are at a different intellectual stage from the under-twos. Babies and young toddlers make social invitations without spoken language, because they do not yet have that facility. Once

Hamid is not being rude, he is deaf, and he didn't realise you were speaking to him.

recognisable words become part of the play and social conversation experience, it is usually obvious to the children when one of their number is speaking but cannot be understood by their peers. If there is any doubt – for instance a young child announces that "Sergio talks funny" – then one of your team needs to be quick to explain that Sergio is speaking Italian, a different language from English.

Disability and ill health

A considerable range of disabilities can affect children in their early years. Of course, there is no simple cause-and-effect for the impact on social interaction and play.

For instance, children who live with chronic ill health may have severe bouts of illness, or periods in hospital, which disrupt the friendships they have successfully made in playgroup. Young children who live with a physical disability could most need an environment that allows them easy access and mobility around the spaces and from indoors to outdoors. They may benefit from simple explanations, given to their peers by an adult who

Links to your practice

Some children will need additional support, but these special extras rest upon clear understanding in the team about the usual pattern of child development and the role of a genuinely helpful adult.

In what ways do the practitioners on your team use their skills of informal observation to determine what is happening in play – especially when disputes are simmering? Are they able to make this process very simple when some children behave more like a younger child?

In what ways do the practitioners set a good example to children about how to share out limited resources – as well as ensuring that there are generous supplies whenever that is practical? Do the staff provide a good role model over offering trades or how to do a nice 'no', when you have not yet finished with the red crayon? Are they able to communicate these messages by signing, when appropriate? Are they able to help other children learn a range of useful signing for play with peers who are unable to communicate in words?

Do the practitioners strive to be fair in their dealings with children? For instance, young children sometimes need help for when another child wants to play with them – or continue longer in a game – and they do not want this. Perhaps Winston has been very patient in playing shops with Josie. But Josie cannot play pretend to the same level of complexity and Winston would really like a break to build a den with his friends. He is not being unpleasant or unkind.

models courtesy in reply to "what's the matter with Charlene's legs?", or explains that Hamid is not being rude, he is deaf (and busy with the train set), so did not realise anyone was speaking to him.

Children, who live with disability on the autistic spectrum, can be utterly confused about the ground rules of social play that their three- or four-year-old peers can now happily negotiate. Pretend play can be a closed door to them, because the leap of imagination does not fit how children look at their world. Many young children develop a passionate interest in particular resources or play enterprises. However, the highly focused interests of children, beyond the mild end of the autistic spectrum, can be so specialised as to exclude other children, whose wish to vary the play is unlikely to be welcome.

Studies, like that of Jannik Beyer and Lone Gammeltoft (2000), focus on ways to support children, whose behaviour lies on the autistic spectrum, in learning some of the social give-and-take that is a usual part of play between young children. Michael Gurainick et al. (2007) and Virginia Buysse et al. (2002) both offer studies of friendship patterns of children with and without disabilities. Their practical suggestions are that practitioners need to give deliberate support to children whose disability means they are not as socially competent in the basic rules of play as their peers. It is not the case that inclusion will work some kind of magic on its own.

Supporting development of social skills

Judy Dunn (2004) makes the useful point that children's development of social skills is not the same as forming friendships. Friendship is a special and intimate relationship. She suggests that young children may be very motivated to use their existing social skills with their friends, because they want to be considerate of someone who matters so much to them. She offers food for thought: that friendship is different from being accepted by a group or the general notion of being popular. Dunn also observes that friendships are voluntary: companions are chosen by children themselves – admittedly from what is available to them.

Friendly or friends?

It is considerate of adults to look towards 'buddying-up' older, or sometimes more settled, children with new arrivals. Well handled, this way of easing social interaction can be positive for the child being supported and a source of personal satisfaction for the child offering that support. But buddies organised by adults are not the same as friends. Even when young children volunteer themselves as social support to a child new to the setting, they usually envisage this offer as a temporary friendly gesture. They may want adult help to extricate themselves if the other child now sticks to them like glue. Buddying is a positive social interaction, but it is not the same as forming a friendship.

I think Judy Dunn is right that something more subtle happens on a regular basis between children who have chosen each other as friends. I have observed the three- and four-year-old version of attentive, social communication, when young children bend their head to listen carefully to a peer and comment positively on what someone else has said or done. Generally, you will notice that friends – young and older – will make that much more effort to understand what is going on with a cross or upset friend. A peer, who is not considered to be a friend, might be dismissed more swiftly, as being silly and just plain wrong. Of course, in an emotionally warm environment, young children do sometimes show sensitivity even though they do not feel close to each other. Also, young friends fall out – just as can happen in later childhood, adolescence or adulthood. You will see and hear the emotional distress that follows from "I am not your friend!".

Learning through first-hand experience

This focus on actual relationships is a crucial point for early years practitioners to hold at the top of their mind. There is a wide range of resources that are promoted as supportive of children's social development. Managers and their teams need to be wary of anything that is marketed as the best way to teach children about social skills, empathy, or qualities that show through children's behaviour such as kindness. Some of the resources or guided activities can – in wise adult hands – be an effective support for young children and part of open conversation that helps them to express their own ideas. However, any of these resources or activities will only work as a supplement to adult sensitivity to real events; never as an alternative to this responsiveness.

Early years practitioners need to keep a firm hold on realistic expectations in terms of child development: young children's understanding of their social world and their ability to juggle ideas with thoughts in their head and spoken words. Susan Campbell (2006) stresses that adults often underestimate the ability of

Links to your practice

Judy Dunn (2004) suggests that children's friendships are the arena in which moral and ethical issues first make sense for a child's world. Children care about their friends; they would rather their friend were happy rather than sad. This emotional quality to the relationship supports the development of a moral sensibility in a direct way.

Can you recall times when a young child really seemed to demonstrate through their chosen actions that they were attentive to the needs of another child? Perhaps they told you that the other child 'needs a cuddle', or the first child searched for something, maybe a special item, that would make their peer feel better.

under-fives to talk about what is happening, or has just happened, within direct social interaction. With experience of learning a vocabulary for emotions, young children can become adept (three- and four-year-old style) in voicing how they are feeling, or making a good guess at what they see on the face of their child companion. Susan Campbell points out that those same adults sometimes over-estimate young children's capacity to follow an adult-led, and often abstract, group discussion about feelings and 'what should we do?'.

Dealing with social troubles at the time

Practical ways of dealing with social dilemmas, or raising the possibility of how someone else might feel, are best shown to young children in response to situations that immediately warrant these skills. The HighScope approach to supporting children in dealing with conflict is a very positive option (see page 23). The key feature is that adults hone their own skills of conflict resolution (usually through training) and use them to help children when children are in dispute. The most delay you allow is to enable furious or very distressed children to calm down enough so that they are able to express themselves in words.

Adult attention needs to be mostly on responding appropriately to spontaneous events. Your team will never have to plan for minor disagreements about who had the little broom first. These events are the stuff of childhood, and they sometimes need adult help. Practitioners need to feel confident to wait a little while, to see if children are likely to resolve this dispute over who is to be which character in their favourite pretend play. Sometimes children are clearly working their way towards a resolution that will succeed for them. Practitioners, who are already involved in a game, behave as a good play partner, who is attentive to events and does not impose their own solutions, but can offer an idea. Young children learn within affectionate, personal relationships with adults who matter to them and whom they trust.

Caution about 'teaching' social development

Early years practitioners need to think carefully about their use of what I call 'step-back methods'. By this phrase, I mean planned, adult-led discussion or activities dependent on additional resources, such as stories with a message or a narrative woven around a puppet or doll. Undoubtedly, some young children – even older ones – find it easier to express themselves through a familiar soft toy. Perhaps 'Monkey' says what three-year-old Oliver feels about being told to go away by the children who have claimed the willow shelter as their exclusive territory. Oliver cannot quite voice his distress and sense of unfairness without this support. He is helped to channel his communication through a loved soft toy at the time.

Articulate four- and five-year-olds may gain in understanding through small group exchanges, so long as they are already experienced in talking out their feelings and point of view within the ordinary ups and downs of life with other children. Even potentially

Discussion about visible actions and invisible emotions makes most sense to young children when open, and often lively, discussion happens as part of the event, or very close in time to a disagreement. In this meaningful context, four- and five-year-olds – even some articulate threes – can be forthright and detailed about who did what, including themselves, and why that was, or was not, alright.

■ Are these events noticed within your team and valued as part of social development – even if the children's voices are initially at top volume?

So long as children have had the experience of hearing an emotional vocabulary (from adults in context or older children), they learn to express their emotions in context at the time they experiencing the feelings. Young children voice their own first-hand experience: "I'm cross with you! It was my turn on the special bike" or "'course she's crying – you pinched her'".

■ Are your team noticing what children can do, in a meaningful context? They need to be alert to these events, at least as much as planning a simple exploration around a story or narrative with a puppet character.

useful resources or activities will not help children, if they are left to struggle at the time of real social troubles. Children are deeply unimpressed by adults who believe that these really important issues – to and for children – can be postponed until a more convenient time for the grown-up, like an adult-led group time. It is also inappropriate to raise conflicts between a few children within the public arena of even a small-group circle time.

I think that some developmentally inappropriate expectations have travelled into the early years sector which aim to teach personal and social development, based on a school classroom model. For instance, I would challenge how using emotions cards, pictures or photos is ever likely to promote young children's understanding of feelings. As mentioned on page 5, there is good reason to say that adults cannot recognise more than four specific emotions – perhaps six – by looking at fixed facial expressions. Young children do not have the background experience of adults and they need a meaningful context. If you or your colleagues are hard pressed to interpret the emotion expressed by a stranger in a photograph – let alone some frozen-face dolls I once saw – then young children will certainly be baffled.

> Using the power of narrative wisely

Young children take dolls and puppets with great seriousness. Within their pretend play and linked story making, they create

details of character, back story and current events around their chosen soft toy, doll or puppet. Sensitive early years practitioners have built on children's abiding interest in narrative to introduce ideas and enable children to air opinions through a puppet or doll who appears on a regular basis. So long as the doll or puppet is introduced well, young children seem to take their story to heart. Children accept and extend the narrative, weave in their own experiences and are often keen to resolve problems that the doll faces, or consider which of two options the puppet should take.

Adult plans to build-in young children's flair for pretend need to be linked with sensible expectations for the age group. The main points when carrying out group work with puppets are:

■ Be realistic about how this kind of group social interaction with a puppet is likely to work positively with young children. Adults need to tune-in to the understanding of under fives and the likely level of abstract thought.

■ Under-threes enjoy a good and lively story with a puppet character, but these very young children will not make sense of more abstract exploration of feelings or 'what if..?' scenarios.

■ Keep the groups small: no more than one adult and four children, six at the most. If the group gets any larger, young children cannot see clearly and have to wait too long for their turn to speak. There is only a short gap of time between having a really good idea and needing to say it out loud.

■ Another risk with larger groups of young children is that the adult's attention is spread too thin. There is a tendency for group time to become more about adult talking and telling.

- Keep the group time relatively short – probably no more than 10-15 minutes, unless the children are clearly still engaged.

- The approach is personal: what has happened in this doll's family or practical problems on which the puppet would welcome some advice.

- Ensure that dolls or favourite puppets are never saddled with a miserable back story, nor a succession of events in which other children are nasty to them – especially if the story implies these unkind children are at another local nursery.

- The previous point is especially important if the doll represents a minority ethnic group or has a disability. The aim is that children see shared ground rather than feel sorry for the doll because the storyline has invited their pity.

> ### Familiar and unfamiliar traditions

Young children's understanding of the social world has to start with their personal life and immediate community. Practitioners working with young children need to hold tight to developmentally appropriate expectations. Early childhood is the time when young boys and girls need to gain a positive sense of themselves and family background. They can create the foundations to an outlook that being different in some way is neither better, nor worse, just different. Early childhood is too soon for adults to try to build children's general knowledge about world faiths or a wide range of unfamiliar cultural traditions.

Young children understand family and local community. They make sense of cultural tradition or religious faith insofar as it belongs in their daily personal and social world. The revised Early Learning Goals for Understanding the World in the Early Years Foundation Stage 2012 (for England) offer a more realistic expectation with reference to 'communities and traditions' rather than 'cultures and beliefs'.

Young children need experiences to show the variations from what they, quite reasonably for their age, think is normal family life. Helpful adults comment on what happens, and give simple answers to questions. For instance:

- Hamid's Grandma brings him and picks him up from nursery. Hamid definitely has a Mummy and Daddy, but they both work during the day.

- All of Jessie's relatives live within ten miles of her home and she sees her auntie and cousins most weekends. Liam also has an auntie, uncle and cousins, but he does not see them very often. They live much further away, in Ireland.

- Kayleigh and her family go to church every Sunday, the building that you and the children pass on the way to the library. Satvinder and his family also worship every weekend; they go to the gurdwara, on the other side of town.

For example: partnership with families

In Little Learners Nursery School, I was fortunate to catch a special event. The nursery was celebrating Songkran, Thai New Year, because a boy, whose family originated from Thailand, attends the nursery.

His mother was pleased to be involved in sharing information about and artefacts from the celebration. She had also worked with the nursery's cook to produce a veritable feast for lunch that day. I joined the meal, which was served within the covered, raised platform that forms one area of the garden.

The children were all keen to try the range of dishes. This special meal, along with other experiences and conversations, not just on the one day, made sense of an event that was unfamiliar to most of the children. However, Thai New Year could have meaning because it was part of life for a familiar child and parent.

> ### Food for thought
>
> Never forget that, in the adult social world, people may say firmly that they would behave in this way faced with a given situation or what is definitely the 'right thing to do'. What is said in the abstract, within conversation, is not necessarily what they do in the actual situation.
>
> So, it is hardly likely that young children will show a greater consistency than adults between anticipated and actual behaviour. Children may be utterly authentic in what they say the puppet, or story character, should do or should avoid doing or saying.
>
> Yet, all of that is much harder in the real situation: when someone has jumped the queue, yet again, for the slide, or will not agree with your statement that they are wearing sandals and not shoes.
>
> I listened to the sandal-shoe dispute a few years ago. The experience reminded me that children deserve respect for issues that matter to them. We are unhelpful adults if our first contribution is to disagree that this topic is worthy of raised voices.

Books and websites

- Bee, H., Boyd, D. (2004) *The Developing Child*, Pearson Education.

- Beyer, J., Gammeltoft, L. (2000) *Autism and Play*, Jessica Kingsley.

- Buysse, V., Goldman, B., Skinner, M. (2002) *Setting Effects on Friendship Formation Among Young Children With and Without Disabilities* (available from: www.sbac.edu/~werned/ DATA/RESEARCH/journals/Excep Children/friendship and young children.pdf).

- Campbell, S. (2006) *Behaviour Problems in Preschool Children: Clinical and Developmental Issues*, The Guildford Press.

- Casey, T. (2005) *Inclusive Play: Practical Strategies for Working with Children ages 3-8*, Paul Chapman Publishing.

- Clifford-Poston, A. (2007) *When Harry Hit Sally: Understanding your child's behaviour*, Simon and Schuster.

- Community Playthings (2010) *Enabling Play: Planning Environments* and other booklets and DVDs (available from: www.communityplaythings.co.uk).

- Danby, S. (2008) 'The value of friends' in: Brooker, L., Woodhead, M., *Developing positive identities: diversity and young children*, The Open University.

- Dorman, H., Dorman, C., (2002) *The Social Toddler: Promoting Positive Behaviour*, The Children's Project.

- Dowling, M. (2005) *Young Children's Personal, Social and Emotional Development*, Paul Chapman Publishing.

- Dunn, J. (1993) *Young Children's Close Relationships Beyond Attachment*, Sage.

- Dunn, J. (2004) *Children's Friendships: The Beginnings of Intimacy*, Blackwell Publishing.

- Eckerman, C. (1993) 'Imitation and toddlers' achievement of co-ordinated actions with others' in: Nadel, J., Camaioni, L., eds. *New Perspectives in Early Communicative Development*, Routledge.

- Eisenberg, N. (1992) *The Caring Child*, Harvard University Press.

- Eliot, L. (2010) *Pink Brain Blue Brain*, Houghton Mifflin Harcourt.

- Evans, B. (2002) *You Can't Come to my Birthday Party: Conflict Resolution with Young Children*, HighScope Press.

- Hope, S. (2007) *A Nurturing Environment for Children up to Three*, Islington Council.

- Garrick, R., Bath, C., Dunn, K., et al (2010) *Children's Experiences of the Early Years Foundation Stage*. Department for Education (available from: www.education. gov.uk/publications/eOrderingDownload/DFE-RR071.pdf).

- Goldman, B., Buyssee, V. (2008) *Making Friends – Assisting Children's Early Friendships*. (available from: www.fpg.unc.edu/~snapshots/snap55.pdf).

- Grieshaber, S., McArdle, F. (2010) *The Trouble with Play*, Open University Press.

- Gurainick, M., Neville, B., Hammond, M. et al (2007) *The Friendships of Young Children with Developmental Delays – A Longitudinal Analysis* (available from: www.ncbi. nlm.nih.gov/pmc/articles/PMC1890038/).

- Gurian, A., Pope, A. (undated) *Do Kids Need Friends?* (available from: www.aboutourkids.org/articles/do_kids_ need_friends).

- Gurian, A., Goodman, R. (undated) *Friends and Friendships* (available from: www.aboutourkids.org/articles/friends_ friendships).

- Hartley-Brewer, E. (2009) *Making Sense of Your Child's Friendships*, Piccadilly Press.

- Hughes, C. (2011) *Social Understanding and Social Lives*, Psychology Press.

- Karmiloff-Smith, A. (1994) *Baby it's You: A Unique Insight into the First Three Years of the Developing Baby*, Ebury Press.

- Lewisham Early Years Advice and Resource Network (2002) *A Place to Learn: Developing a Stimulating Environment*, LEARN.

- Layard, R., Dunn, J. (2009) *A Good Childhood: Values in a Competitive Age* (The report of the Children's Society's Good Childhood Inquiry), Penguin.

Books and websites

- Lindon J (2010a) *Child-initiated Learning: Positive Relationships in the Early Years*, Practical Pre-School Books.

- Lindon J (2010b) *The Key Person Approach: Positive Relationships in the Early Years*, Practical Pre-School Books.

- Lindon J (2011) *Planning for Effective Early Learning: Professional Skills in Developing a Child-centred Approach to Planning*, Practical Pre-School Books.

- Lindon J (2012a) *What Does It Mean to be...?* Series of child development books, each focussing on one year in early childhood, Practical Pre-School Books.

- Lindon J. (2012b) *Equality and Inclusion in Early Childhood*, Hodder Education.

- Lindon J. (2012c) *Understanding Child Development 0-8 years*, Hodder Education.

- Lindon J. (2012d) *Understanding Children's Behaviour 0-11 years*, Hodder Education.

- Murray, L., Andrews, L. (2000) *The Social Baby: Understanding Babies' Communication from Birth*, The Children's Project.

- Nangle, D., Erdley, C. eds. (2001) *The Role of Friendship in Psychological Adjustment*, Jossey Bass.

- Paley, V. G. (1992) *You Can't Say You Can't Play*, University of Chicago Press.

- Paley, V. G. (2004) *A Child's Work: the Importance of Fantasy Play*, University of Chicago Press.

- Rich, D., Casanova, D., Dixon, A. et al (2005) *First Hand Experience: What Matters to Children*, Rich Learning Opportunities.

- Siren Films (2008) *Falling Out, The Wonder Year*, Siren Films.

- Vallotton, C., Ayoub, C. (2010) *Use your words: do expressive language skills help toddlers self-regulate?* (available from: <http://news.msu.edu/media/documents/2010/09/0fb3ad11-b38c-4c1e-9996-05e2615e2b7a.pdf).

- Williams, L. (2010) *Am I staying for lunch today?* (available from: www.ncb.org.uk/PDF/Exec Summary Free Entitlement.pdf).

Acknowledgements

My heartfelt thanks to the managers and teams of these settings who made me so welcome and agreed to using examples from my visit: Little Learners Nursery School (Skegness), Oakfield Nursery School (Altrincham) and Red Hen Day Nursery (Legbourne). A big thank you to the children in these settings, who were friendly to a visitor and keen to show and explain things to me. Any children, or staff, mentioned in the examples have been given alternative names.

The content of this book has undoubtedly been influenced by the excellent practice I observed in visits to other settings within recent years. I am especially appreciative of what I learned during time spent in the settings thanked in other titles I have written for Practical Pre-School Books – especially *Child-Initiated Learning* (2010a) and *Planning for Effective Early Learning* (2011).